Counselling: Philosophical?

Awakening Socrates in You

Counselling: Philosophical?

Awakening Socrates in You

Deepanwita Dutta

**MOTILAL BANARSIDASS INTERNATIONAL
DELHI**

First Edition : Delhi, 2024

© MOTILAL BANARSIDASS INTERNATIONAL
All Rights Reserved

ISBN : 978-93-48128-37-9 (PB)
ISBN : 978-93-48128-52-2 (HB)

Also available at :
MOTILAL BANARSIDASS INTERNATIONAL
41 U.A. Bungalow Road, (Back Lane) Jawahar Nagar, Delhi-110007
4261/3 (Basement), Ansari Road, Darya Ganj, New Delhi-110002
Shop#. 6, 241, Luz Ginza Complex, Luz Corner, Mylapore, Chennai - 600004
12/1A, 2nd Floor, Bankim Chatterjee Street, Kolkata - 700073

Stockist : Motilal Books, Ashok Rajpath, Near Kali Mandir, Patna-800004

No part of this book may be reproduced in any form or by any electronic or mechanical means including information storage and retrieval systems without permission in writing from the publishers, except by a reviewer who may quote brief passages in a review.

Printed in India by
MOTILAL BANARSIDASS INTERNATIONAL

Dedicated to

My teachers of Philosophy

Acknowledgement

This is my first book, and writing it has been a transformative journey filled with discovery and personal growth. Along the way, I've been fortunate to receive guidance and support from many remarkable individuals, to whom I'm deeply grateful.

First, my heartfelt thanks to the Philosophical Practitioners' Association of India (PPAI) and its founders. Their dedication to making philosophical practice a part of everyday life has been a constant source of inspiration. The knowledge and insights they've shared have been invaluable throughout this journey.

To my friend and fellow research scholar, whose introduction to PPAI and encouragement to attend their workshop was a turning point in my philosophical exploration. I am thankful for the doors he opened.

I am deeply grateful to my professors at the University of North Bengal for nurturing my academic growth over the past few years. Their guidance has been instrumental in shaping my intellectual development.

I am equally indebted to the many philosophical practitioners and scholars whose wisdom has shaped this work. Their insights and contributions have provided a solid foundation upon which this book stands.

Finally, I owe a special thanks to my mentor, Prof. J. C. Basak. His unwavering belief in me, along with his profound expertise and consistent guidance, has been crucial in turning this idea into a reality. Without his guidance, this book would not exist in its current form.

Preface

I still remember my days in secondary school, when I was weighed down by questions that seemed impossible to answer. Who am I? What am I really doing here? What's the purpose of all this? Life felt like a jigsaw puzzle with pieces that didn't fit, leaving me more confused. During those years, existential questions followed me everywhere, clouding my thoughts. Then, I stumbled upon a book that changed everything—a lifeline that opened the door to a world where my questions were not only asked but explored deeply. This was my first encounter with philosophy, and it felt like a revelation.

As I continued through secondary school, I excelled academically, particularly in the sciences, where I received a great deal of encouragement to pursue a conventional career path. But despite this, I felt an irresistible pull toward something beyond the empirical realm. My stubborn resistance to the conventional path wasn't just a phase—it was a deep, unyielding quest to understand reality at its core. And so, I embarked on a journey with philosophy as my guide.

However, as I delved deeper into this subject, pursuing it academically for nearly a decade, I noticed something troubling. The lively debates and the passionate exploration of ideas that had first drawn me to philosophy seemed to have been replaced by dry, academic exercises. Philosophy, once a vibrant guide to living a thoughtful, examined life, had become confined to the sterile environment of classrooms and academic papers. It felt as though the heartbeat of philosophy had been silenced, its connection to everyday life severed.

This realization was disheartening, but it also ignited a new resolve within me: to revive the living spirit of philosophy and make it relevant to our daily struggles and decisions. What if philosophy could be more than just an academic pursuit? What if it could be a practical tool, guiding us through the complexities of real life?

This resolve led me to the field of philosophical counselling, a practice that seeks to bridge the gap between philosophical thought and practical life. Philosophical counselling is not about abstract theories or esoteric debates; it's about applying the wisdom of philosophy to tackle real-life challenges—whether it's a career crossroads, a relationship dilemma, or finding meaning in the face of adversity.

So, why should you read this book? Why invest your time and attention in it? Because this isn't just another book on philosophy—it's an invitation to embark on a journey, your journey. This book seeks to bridge the gap between the philosophical ideas that have shaped human thought for centuries and the real-life challenges we face today.

Have you ever felt a deep yearning for something more meaningful than the daily grind? Have you ever questioned the path you're on, wondering if there's something richer, deeper, waiting just beyond the horizon? This book dares to ask those questions and more. It challenges you to think, to question, and to discover the tools that have been honed over millennia to help us live more meaningful, purposeful lives.

I don't pretend to have all the answers and I'm far from an authority on all things. What I offer here is my own exploration, my attempt to bring philosophy back into the flow of everyday life. My hope is that as you turn the pages, you'll find ideas and insights that resonate with your own experiences, that help you navigate your own journey. Together, let's rekindle the flame of inquiry and bring wisdom back to where it belongs—into our daily choices, challenges, and triumphs.

Deepanwita Dutta

Contents

	Page
Acknowledgement	(vii)
Preface	(ix)
Chapter-1 : Introduction: Philosophy in Action: A Story Unfolds	1
Chapter-2 : Philosophical Counselling: A New Path to Clarity and Meaning	17
Chapter-3 : Historical and Ancient Roots of Philosophical Counselling	31
Chapter-4 : Fundamental Approaches and Methods in Philosophical Counselling	43
Chapter-5 : Key Stages of Philosophical Counselling	58
Chapter-6 : Exploring Methods and Practices in Indian Philosophy	66
Chapter-7 : Addressing Life's Common Philosophical Dilemmas	84
Chapter-8 : Major Criticisms and Challenges of Philosophical Counselling	94
Chapter-9 : Conclusion: The Future of Philosophical Counselling in India	98
Further Readings	102
Index	108

Chapter - 1

Philosophy in Action: A Story Unfolds

Let me take you back to the heart of the city, a place where skyscrapers stretch upwards like the ambitions of its people, and the hum of technology fills every corner. In this concrete jungle, amidst the relentless pace of modern life, lived a man named Rohan. On the surface, Rohan was the epitome of success—a digital marketing expert with a promising career, a man who seemed to have it all. But beneath this polished exterior lay a different story, one of quiet desperation and an overwhelming sense of emptiness.

Rohan's life was a blur of meetings, deadlines, and relentless striving, like a machine set on autopilot. Each day bled into the next, each achievement feeling like a step on a treadmill—moving but never progressing. Despite his professional success, he was haunted by a gnawing void—a void that no amount of accolades or financial rewards could fill. It was as if he were a character in a play, performing his lines and hitting his marks, but disconnected from the deeper meaning of the story.

For months, Rohan sought solace in psychological counselling, bravely confronting the stigma that often surrounds mental health issues. His therapist listened patiently, offered coping strategies, and provided a sympathetic ear. But no matter how much he talked, no matter how diligently he practised the techniques, the core of his distress remained untouched—like trying to treat the symptoms of a disease without addressing its *cause*. His struggle was not one of mental illness but of a philosophical crisis—a crisis that no amount of psychotherapy could resolve.

One night, after another unfulfilling day at work, Rohan found himself mindlessly scrolling through the internet, searching for something—anything—that might provide a distraction. It's a familiar scene: we scroll endlessly, moving from one dopamine hit to the next, hoping that the next video or reel will satisfy an urge we can't quite describe. But what we're really looking for is clarity—a spark of insight.

What Rohan found instead was a forum where people shared their existential struggles, their philosophical musings, and their quests for meaning. Intrigued, Rohan clicked on a blog post titled "Finding Meaning in a Chaotic World". The questions it posed struck him like a sudden gust of wind that shakes a stagnant sail: *"What is my life for? What does it mean to live a good life? How do I find meaning in a world that seems indifferent?"*

Hooked by these significant inquiries, Rohan clicked on a recommendation for an e-book on philosophy. He downloaded it and began reading, diving into questions like, *"Why do I feel so disconnected despite being surrounded by people?"* and *"What is my true identity beyond my social roles?"* These questions struck at the very core of his being. As he continued, he found himself confronted by even deeper existential dilemmas: *"Is life inherently absurd, or does it hold a hidden meaning? Am I living an authentic life, or merely conforming to societal expectations? What does it mean to be true to myself, and how do I navigate the pressures to fit into societal molds? In a world where I am free to choose my path, how do I ensure my choices reflect my true self? What is the nature of my consciousness, and how do I reconcile the transient nature of life with the desire for permanence and stability?"* These were deep questions that reverberated to the core of Rohan's being and which propelled him into this journey of self-discovery. These questions were fundamentally different from those explored in his psychological sessions. They were not about managing symptoms or altering behaviours; they were about understanding the very essence of his existence. Rohan realized that his struggle was not about a mental health disorder, but about wrestling with profound philosophical questions.

Rohan's life story, his existential crisis, and his boredom reflect a universal experience. Many of us go through the motions of daily life, fulfilling our roles and responsibilities, yet feeling an undercurrent of dissatisfaction and questioning the deeper meaning of our existence.

Rohan's journey is, in many ways, ours journey.

Strange but true, one can lead an entire life without ever resolving these questions. What a profound tragedy it is—to exist without truly living, to drift through life that is unexamined. As Socrates once famously affirmed, "The unexamined life is not worth living."

Reflection Exercise for You

Take a moment to reflect on your own life. What are the questions that keep you awake during moments of quiet reflection? What doubts or uncertainties linger in your thoughts throughout the day? Write them down. These questions mark the beginning of your journey. As you continue through this book, keep these questions close—they will serve as your compass as you navigate the philosophical insights and tools that follow.

Now, let's imagine a different story. Picture yourself in a dialogue with a trained philosophical practitioner, who acts as a mirror, reflecting your thoughts back to you in sharper focus, helping you to question, analyse, and understand the core of your being. This process illuminates your path, enabling you to recognize the values that truly matter to you and to align your actions with these values.

Instead of wandering through life aimlessly like a boat without a rudder, you begin to live with intention and clarity. Your sense of purpose becomes clearer, and you start to experience a profound connection to your existence. This transformation is not just about solving problems but about embracing a more thoughtful and meaningful approach to life. By engaging with philosophical practices, you gain the tools to deal with life's complexities with wisdom and insight, leading to a more fulfilling and authentic existence.

In this book, we invite you to embark on a transformative journey—where philosophy becomes a living, breathing guide to handling life's complexities. Together, we will explore the timeless wisdom of philosophical practices, delving into their principles, methodologies, and real-world applications. This is not just a collection of abstract concepts or academic theories but a practical roadmap that can profoundly impact your life. Whether you're searching for clarity, grappling with difficult decisions, or seeking a deeper understanding of yourself, the tools and insights presented here can help you uncover truths that resonate on both personal and universal levels.

As J. Krishnamurti once said, *"To understand yourself is the beginning of wisdom."*[1] This idea forms the foundation of our exploration. Philosophy, at its core, is about more than pondering lofty questions in distant ivory towers. It is about applying tested wisdom to everyday challenges. From

---

1 Krishnamurti. J. (2004). *Freedom From The Known*. Krishnamurti Foundation India. P. 6.

ancient Eastern philosophies to modern existential thought, which have stood the test of time, we will explore how these frameworks offer solutions to contemporary dilemmas. This journey is about equipping you with practical tools that address the unique struggles you face—whether they involve questions of identity, purpose, or personal values.

Through engaging dialogues, reflective exercises, and thought-provoking questions, this book provides a comprehensive roadmap for your own journey of self-discovery. You will learn how to engage with life's biggest philosophical questions and how to apply them to your personal experiences.

As you progress through the chapters, remember that the journey of philosophical inquiry is deeply personal and unique to each individual. The insights you uncover will be your own, shaped by your values, beliefs, and life experiences. Embrace this journey with an open heart and a curious mind, and you will discover the profound impact that philosophical reflection can have on how you live, think, and feel.

The Pulse of Philosophy:

Understanding what philosophy signifies extends far beyond its academic and etymological definitions. Etymologically, philosophy has been described as the love of wisdom or the quest for knowledge, a pursuit that is often associated with deep contemplation and abstract thinking. However, this is only a narrow view of what philosophy truly encompasses. In reality, philosophy has been understood and practised in diverse ways across cultures and historical periods. It is not merely an intellectual exercise or a theoretical discipline confined to universities and scholars. Instead, philosophy has been conceptualized as a 'way of life', it is deeply rooted in the lived experiences of human beings. It is concerned with how we live our lives, how we interact with others, and how we make sense of our existence. It helps us to 'be' in different ways, depending on how we conceptualize life. To be philosophical is to live with awareness and intentionality. To live, in this sense, is to act and react to the world around us, to engage with the 'other'—whether that other is a person, an idea, or a situation. Through our actions and reactions, we make choices that assert our existence and shape our being.

In the Indian tradition, philosophy is referred to as *Darshana*, which means 'a way of seeing' or 'a way of conceptualizing'. This concept emphasizes that philosophy is about how we perceive and interpret the world around us, guiding our actions and decisions. Moreover, it is recognized as a life-changing and transformative tool. Philosophy is not just about understanding the world but about transforming ourselves through that understanding. It offers frameworks for addressing life's fundamental questions, helping us to make sense of our experiences and navigate the challenges we encounter. It also serves as a problem-solving device, providing us with the intellectual tools to approach and find an answer to the dilemmas we face.[1]

However, over the years, philosophy has become an almost purely academic discipline detached from day-to-day personal concerns. Although philosophy is quintessential for understanding the fundamental nature of knowledge, however, its application is largely absent from public discourse. Despite the growing quest for knowledge, philosophy is being reduced to the academic world with its basic forms of teaching and research. On account of this

---

1 Devarakonda, B. (2021). Shifts in the Classical Indian Conception of Philosophical Practice: *Vedic, Itihāsa-purāṇic,* and *Dārśanic. Philosophical Practice: Journal of the APPA, 16*(1), 2602-2609, pp. 2602-2603.

desideratum, there is a pressing need to integrate it into broader public understanding in a more impactful way.

What Does It Mean to Be Philosophical?

To be philosophical is to embark on the journey of an examined life—a path of deep inquiry into the fundamental questions that shape human existence, knowledge, values, and reality. It's more than just thinking; it's a way of engaging with life, driven by curiosity and a profound desire to understand not only the world but our place within it.

Philosophy invites us to examine our motivations, desires, and fears, offering a mirror through which we see ourselves more clearly. This self-awareness cultivates authenticity, allowing us to live in alignment with our true values rather than bending to societal expectations. Living authentically means making choices that reflect who we genuinely are, not who we're told to be.

Self-discovery, sparked by philosophical inquiry, pushes us to reflect on our purpose. It urges us to set meaningful goals that give life direction and motivate us to act with intention. By wrestling with questions of existence, morality, and values, we find not only answers but also meaning—a sense of purpose that infuses our experiences with greater depth and fulfilment.

Philosophy is also an ethical compass. It prompts us to consider the moral weight of our actions, fostering a sense of responsibility towards ourselves and the world around us. This reflection enhances our ability to contribute positively to society, making us more compassionate and aware of the impact we have on others.

In the face of life's challenges, the habit of philosophical reflection builds resilience. It teaches us to embrace adversity as a source of growth, allowing us to navigate uncertainty with calm and clarity. As we continuously reassess our beliefs in light of new experiences, we become more adaptable, flexible in our thinking, and open to change.

Ultimately, being philosophical is a lifelong process of personal growth. It's about striving toward your highest potential, one moment of reflection at a time. Over the years, this practice of self-examination transforms into wisdom—an enduring understanding of life that goes beyond mere knowledge. Through philosophy, we don't just learn about the world; we learn how to live in it with purpose, meaning, and integrity.

> **Exercise 1: The Examined Life – Reflection Journal**
>
> Take time each day for one week to reflect on your daily actions, decisions, and interactions. Choose one or two specific moments from each day and explore the following questions in your journal:

1. **What were the driving motivations behind my actions?**
   - Did I act out of habit, fear, social expectation, or alignment with my personal values?

Note: All visuals used in this book are generated by AI.

- Did my emotions (stress, joy, anger etc.) influence my decision in this moment?

2. **How did my actions impact others and myself?**
   - Did I bring value, connection, or clarity to those around me?
   - Did my actions serve my growth and well-being, or did they detract from them?

3. **What alternative choices could I have made?**
   - Consider how you might approach the situation differently next time. Would you have chosen differently if you had taken more time to reflect or paused before reacting?

4. **How can I bring more intentionality to my future actions?**
   - What small changes can you implement to align your daily actions with your long-term values and beliefs?

Goal: At the end of the week, review your journal entries and look for patterns. Reflect on what you've learned about your motivations, values, and areas of growth. How has this process of self-examination helped you gain insight into your life?

By examining life through a philosophical lens, we unearth ourselves. Neuroscientific research substantiates this process, revealing that neuroplasticity allows the brain to change and adapt based on new experiences and reflections. As we engage in philosophical inquiry, we're not only changing our minds—we're literally rewiring our brains, reinforcing the possibility of growth and self-improvement throughout life. This means that personal growth and philosophical inquiry are not just theoretical—they physically reshape the brain, reinforcing new patterns of thinking and behaviour.

As these new pathways form, we deepen our understanding of the values that truly define us. This process allows us to live authentically—making choices that reflect who we truly are, rather than conforming to societal pressures. This authenticity becomes a compass, guiding us toward a life filled with purpose and intentionality.

Jean-Paul Sartre offers a powerful reminder of the importance of this freedom in our lives: "Man is condemned to be free; because once thrown into the world, he is responsible for everything he does."[1] The choices we make must align with our highest ideals and deepest values if we are to live meaningfully.

> **Exercise 2: Aligning Actions with Values**
> Take a quiet moment to reflect on a recent significant decision or choice you made—whether in your career, relationships, or personal life. Explore the following questions:

1. **What values were at the core of this decision?**
   - Were you motivated by values such as authenticity, compassion, honesty, or personal growth? Or did external factors like fear of judgment or social pressure influence your decision?

2. **If this choice didn't fully align with your values, why?**
   - Reflect on what got in the way. Did time pressure, fear of conflict, or a need to please others lead you away from what felt right for you?

3. **What would it look like to make decisions that are fully aligned with your true values?**
   - Visualize what such decisions might feel like. How

---

[1] Sartre, J. P. (1957). *Being and Nothingness: An Essay on Phenomenological Ontology* (H. E. Barnes, Trans.). Methuen & Co. Ltd. p. 553.

would your relationships, work, or personal life change if you consistently acted from a place of inner alignment?

4. **Action Step:** Make a commitment to align your next significant choice with your values.

   • Identify a decision you will soon need to make and outline how you will approach it differently, ensuring your values guide your actions.

Goal: By focusing on aligning your daily decisions with your core values, you'll create a life that feels more authentic and intentional. Return to this exercise regularly to check in with yourself.

The Unexamined Life

In contrast, an unexamined life is a life lived on autopilot—where deep reflection is absent, and actions are driven by unconscious forces. Without questioning our motivations or beliefs, we become trapped in habitual behaviours, which neuroscience shows are controlled by neural circuits in the basal ganglia. These circuits become stronger the more they are reinforced. Reflective questioning breaks these automatic patterns by encouraging  self-awareness and intentional action, helping individuals rewire their brains and regain control over their choices and behaviours. When we fail to engage in such reflection, we drift through life without a clear sense of purpose or direction. An unexamined life is often marked by a profound disconnection from our true selves, leading to a sense of emptiness and meaninglessness.

Without self-reflection, we may find ourselves conforming to external pressures, making choices that do not align with our values, and ultimately living inauthentically. The absence of critical thinking and ethical reflection can lead to moral ambiguity, where we fail to take responsibility for our actions or consider the impact we have on others.

Living without reflection also leaves us more vulnerable to adversity. Without the resilience that comes from regularly reassessing our beliefs and actions, we struggle to adapt to life's inevitable changes. Instead of learning and growing, we remain stagnant, unable to break free from old patterns or develop a deeper understanding of ourselves and the world around us.

In essence, the unexamined life is a life lived without awareness, fulfilment, or growth. It lacks the richness that comes from living with purpose, intention, and a deep connection to our true selves.

> ### Exercise 3: Breaking Free from Autopilot
>
> For three days, consciously observe moments when you feel like you are operating on "autopilot"—moments when you act without reflection or awareness. Keep a journal where you answer these questions each evening:

1. **Identify moments of automatic behaviour:**
   - Did you respond to an email, complete a task, or make a decision without much thought? What actions seemed mechanical?

2. **What external forces or habits drove these actions?**
   - Were your actions driven by pressure, routine, or urgency? What deeper motivations might have been at play, and how did they affect your choices?
3. **How did these autopilot moments align with your values?**
   - Did these automatic actions serve your long-term goals, or were they just reflexive reactions? How can you approach these situations with more awareness and intention in the future?
4. **Action Step**: Consciously pause before one daily action:
   - Before responding to a task or decision tomorrow? pause for a few seconds and ask yourself: What am I about to do, and why? Is this choice aligned with my core values?

Exercise 4: Mindfulness Practice – Cultivating Awareness

Mindfulness is a powerful tool for becoming more aware of your thoughts, feelings and actions without getting lost in them. For this exercise, find a quiet space and follow these steps:

---

1. **Find a comfortable position**—either seated or lying down.
   - Close your eyes and take a few deep breaths. Focus on the sensation of your breath as it enters and leaves your body.
2. **Begin to notice your thoughts.**
   - As thoughts arise, simply observe them without judgment. Don't try to change them or push them away. Acknowledge each thought and gently return your focus to your breath.

3. **Practice detachment from your thoughts.**
   - Imagine each thought as a cloud drifting by in the sky. Observe it and let it pass, without engaging or getting attached to it.
4. **Continue this for 5–10 minutes.**
   - When you finish, reflect on how the experience felt. Did you notice any patterns in your thoughts? Were there any recurring themes?

Goal: Regular mindfulness practice allows you to become more attuned to your inner life, cultivating a deeper sense of awareness and calm. At the end of the week, review your journal entries and identify any recurring patterns. Neuroscientific studies show that mindfulness and reflective journaling engage the brain's prefrontal cortex, strengthening the neural pathways that regulate emotional responses. This makes it easier to navigate life's challenges with greater clarity and composure. Over time, this practice will help you respond to difficulties thoughtfully and intentionally, rather than reacting impulsively.

The Journey Ahead

Throughout life, we encounter an array of challenges—whether they stem from existential crises, moral dilemmas, major life decisions, or personal questions of identity and self-understanding. The weight of these challenges can feel overwhelming, particularly when we lack the tools to address them.

From chronic stress and anxiety to interpersonal conflicts and uncertainty about the future, life presents no shortage of struggles. Yet, superficial solutions often fall short. Instead, these moments call for deep philosophical reflection—an inquiry into the core of who we are and how we can live in alignment with our highest truths.

In the following chapters, we will explore how philosophical practices can serve as powerful tools to address these challenges, guiding us toward a more authentic, meaningful, and fulfilling existence. This book is an invitation to look beyond the surface and dive deeply into the questions that matter most. It is a journey not just of thought, but of transformation—one that has the potential to reshape the way you live, one intentional, thoughtful step at a time.

> **Exercise 5: Facing Life's Challenges with Reflection**
>
> Think of a challenge you're currently facing. It could be related to your career, personal life, or relationships. Use the following steps to apply philosophical reflection to the situation:

1. **Identify the core philosophical question behind the challenge:**
   - Is the challenge about identity, values, purpose, or ethics?
2. **Reflect on different philosophical perspectives:**
   - Choose a philosophical framework to apply to this challenge:
   - **Stoicism**: How can you focus on what is within your control and accept what is outside of it?
   - **Existentialism**: How can you create meaning in this situation through your choices?
   - **Eastern philosophy**: How might letting go of attachments and expectations ease your struggle?
   - In the chapters ahead, we will delve deep into a broader range of philosophical tools, drawing from both Western and Eastern traditions, to deepen your understanding and offer practical insights.

3. **Consider how this challenge can be an opportunity for growth:**
   - Instead of seeing this challenge as an obstacle, how might it serve as a catalyst for personal growth, deeper understanding, or change? What lessons can you learn from it?
4. **Action Step:** Create a practical plan to address the challenge:
   - Based on your reflection, outline one or two actions you can take that are aligned with your philosophical perspective. How will you approach this challenge differently tomorrow?

Goal

By using philosophical reflection to face your challenges, you'll find a new sense of clarity, strength, and resilience in your ability to navigate adversity.

Chapter - 2

Philosophical Counselling: A Path to Clarity and Meaning

You've arrived here not by accident, but through the natural evolution of your own search for meaning. Much like how we gradually realize the need for a deeper purpose—perhaps after years of chasing professional achievements or after personal milestones leave us feeling unfulfilled—philosophical Counselling arises when we start asking questions that go beyond daily routines. This process of self-inquiry is often triggered by a life event: a career accomplishment that feels unfulfilling, a relationship that feels stagnant, or even the sense of being stuck in the same loop of habits. These moments push us toward a new kind of guidance—*philosophical counselling*—a unique blend of ancient wisdom and modern support that helps you navigate the complexities of existence with clarity and insight.

Welcome to Philosophical Counselling: A New World Awaits

Philosophical counselling stands at the intersection of thought and action, where philosophy transforms from an abstract discipline into a deeply personal, practical tool for self-examination and growth. It's a process that doesn't just engage the mind—it stirs the heart, prompting you to explore your inner world. Here, we don't merely ponder life's questions; we confront them head-on, with the aim of emerging wiser, more self-aware, and more in tune with our values.

For example, imagine a successful entrepreneur feeling unfulfilled despite financial success. In a philosophical Counselling session, rather than addressing symptoms of anxiety or stress, the focus might shift to questions like, *"What does success mean to you? Are you living in alignment with your deeper values?"* Through such inquiry, the client might uncover that their dissatisfaction stems from pursuing goals set by societal standards, not their own.

But what exactly is counselling? To truly understand this evolving practice, we must revisit the roots of the word itself. Derived from the Latin *consilium*, meaning "advice" or "consultation", it emphasizes the collaborative nature of the counselling process. At its core, *consilium* signifies "making decisions together", reflecting the shared journey between counsellor and counselee. Counselling is more than just getting advice—it's about working together to explore ideas and make choices that transform how we live.

Philosophical Counselling: A Journey of Self-exploration

Philosophical counselling, still an emerging field, adds a unique layer to the practice of counselling by focusing on existential and philosophical concerns. Imagine you're someone who's followed all the rules of success—graduating with honours, climbing the corporate ladder, and buying the dream house—yet still feel a sense of dissatisfaction creeping in. You start asking yourself: *Why am I doing all of this? What does it really mean to live a fulfilling life?* These are not problems a typical therapy session will always tackle directly, but philosophical counselling dives into the heart of such questions. It offers something beyond the traditional scope of psychological therapy, inviting individuals to engage in a reflective process that explores the very foundations of their beliefs, assumptions, and values.

Imagine sitting across from a counsellor, not to discuss mental health *per se*, but to dive into a conversation about your worldview—your sense of purpose, your ethical dilemmas, your concept of meaning. Here, clients aren't looking for symptom relief; they are seeking answers to their profound questions.

For instance, someone struggling with career choices might use philosophical counselling to ask themselves deeper questions: *"What kind of life do I want to lead? What do I value more—security or personal freedom?"* Such sessions go beyond career counselling and touch on the client's core values, reshaping how they perceive their life's direction.

A Reflective Process for Self-Reliance

In philosophical counselling, the counsellor acts less as a problem solver and more as a guide through deep introspection. Through thought-provoking dialogue, clients are encouraged to reflect on their life choices, examine their values, and explore the principles guiding their actions. The counsellor doesn't offer ready-made solutions but instead helps clients unearth the assumptions and beliefs shaping their worldview. It's like shining a flashlight into the dark chambers of

your mind, illuminating the thoughts and assumptions you didn't even realize were there.

As an illustration, a client dealing with relationship struggles might approach a philosophical counsellor not for advice on how to fix the relationship but to explore the deeper question: *"What does love mean to me? How do I balance personal freedom with commitment?"* Through this process, they might realize that their dissatisfaction stems from a fundamental mismatch between their values and expectations.

The ultimate goal of philosophical counselling is *self-reliance*—the ability to critically think about your life and apply philosophical insights on your own. Much like a gym trainer who teaches you how to work out properly, the counsellor equips you with techniques to strengthen your own philosophical 'muscles'. They guide you through exercises that help you build the mental discipline needed to examine your life, but it's you who ultimately lift the weight. Over time, you don't just rely on the trainer for every session; you gain the confidence and ability to maintain your own growth and make decisions independently. Clients leave philosophical counselling not only with answers but also with the tools to continue asking the right questions long after the sessions have ended.

The Debate: Wisdom or Well-being? The Core Aim of Philosophical Counselling

Philosophical counselling stirs debate among practitioners about its core aim. Should the primary goal be well-being, as it often is in psychological counselling? Or is it, as thinkers like Prof. Ran Lahav[1] and Prof. Lou

---

1 Prof. Ran Lahav is an Israeli-born American philosopher who developed philosophical activities for the general public. He is a Philosophical Counsellor, Philosophical Practitioner, and University teacher of philosophy and psychology.

Marinoff[1] suggest, the pursuit of *philosophical wisdom*, with well-being emerging as a by-product? It's a bit like asking whether the goal of a journey is the destination or the knowledge gained along the way—sometimes, they're inseparable.

Prof. Balaganapathi[2] argues that the essence of philosophical counselling lies in developing self-reliance through philosophical insight.[3] It's not about feeling better—it's about becoming better equipped to understand and navigate the world through reason, introspection, and self-awareness. Consider someone who comes into Counselling feeling lost in life. Rather than focusing on short-term relief, philosophical Counselling might guide them through the process of crafting a life philosophy—one that helps them frame life's inevitable hardships in a way that provides meaning. While psychological Counselling may address immediate distress, philosophical Counselling focuses on long-term transformation. Hence, the debate underscores a powerful truth: philosophical counselling doesn't seek to comfort—it seeks to illuminate.

---

1 Lou Marinoff is a professor at the City College of New York (CCNY) in the Department of Philosophy and Asian Studies and the founding president of the American Philosophical Practitioners Association (APPA).

2 A professor at the University of Delhi in the Department of Philosophy, and a founding member of the Philosophical Practitioners Association of India (PPAI).

3 Devarakonda, B., & Baniwal, V. (2023). Conversations on Psychological Counselling and Philosophical Counselling: Examining the Convergences and Divergences Between Philosophical and Psychological Counselling. *Philosophical Practice: Journal of the APPA, 18*(1), 3072-3084. p. 3073.

Why Philosophical Counselling? When to Seek This Path?

Why turn to philosophical counselling when psychological counselling already exists? Psychology, once a branch of philosophy, evolved into its own discipline by adopting scientific methods to understand the mind and behaviour. Psychology mainly focuses on mental health, using tested methods to diagnose and treat psychological issues.

Philosophical counselling, however, addresses issues that are *philosophical at their core*: existential doubt, ethical dilemmas, personal values, and life purpose. As Lou Marinoff suggests, philosophical counselling helps people explore moral conflicts, metaphysical questions, and personal values—these aren't psychological disorders but deep philosophical concerns that require a different kind of reflection—one rooted in the exploration of ideas and values rather than mental health diagnoses. It's like addressing the roots of a tree instead of pruning the branches—you go to the source of growth and strength.

Prof. Devarakonda points out that philosophical counselling is best suited for individuals who are rational and functional, yet seek deeper clarity and self-understanding.[1] It is not a replacement for psychological therapy, especially when medical intervention is required. Rather, philosophical counselling complements psychological counselling by addressing the questions of meaning, ethics, and self-discovery that traditional therapy might overlook.

Where Philosophy and Psychology Meet—And Where They Diverge

While both philosophical and psychological counselling share the goal of improving the client's quality of life, they

---

1 Ibid. p. 3075.

diverge in their approaches and outcomes. To understand how these two disciplines intersect and differ, let's explore their common ground as well as their unique pathways.

Convergence: Shared Goals

1. **Active Listening and Empathy:** Both philosophical and psychological counselling rely on creating a supportive, empathetic environment. Whether the focus is on existential questions or emotional well-being, the counsellor listens deeply and without judgment, ensuring the client feels heard, understood, and respected. It's akin to offering a mirror in which the client can see themselves more clearly, with the counsellor's reflection helping to guide the process.

2. **Improvement of Life:** Both forms of counselling seek to enhance the client's well-being. While psychological counselling often tirelessly aims for mental health improvements, philosophical counselling helps individuals find coherence and meaning by examining their beliefs, values, and purpose.

Imagine a client dealing with anxiety about life transitions. A psychologist might focus on managing anxiety symptoms through approaches such as psychoanalysis, psychodynamic, Cognitive Behavioural Therapy (CBT) and so on, while a philosophical counsellor might ask, *"What is your fear rooted in? Is it the fear of change, or perhaps the fear of losing control over your future?"* By examining these deeper questions, the client may gain a more profound understanding of the anxiety's existential root.

Divergence: Different Approaches

1. **Focus and Scope:** Philosophical counselling is concerned with life's *big questions*: *"What is the meaning*

of life? What is a good life?" and so on. It is a broad exploration of beliefs and values, well-suited to those seeking clarity on philosophical and existential issues. Psychological counselling, on the other hand, addresses mental health challenges like anxiety, depression, or trauma. Its scope is narrower, aiming for functional improvements in daily life through empirically tested methods.

2. **Techniques and Modalities:** Philosophical counselling draws on methods like Socratic dialogue and logical analysis, encouraging reflection, critical thinking, and self-discovery. It is not about symptom relief—it is about understanding the philosophical foundations of one's life. Psychological counselling applies evidence-based techniques such as psychoanalysis[1], psychodynamic therapy[2], Cognitive Behavioural Therapy (CBT)[3], Rational Emotive Behavioural Therapy (REBT)[4],

---

1 Psychoanalysis is a therapeutic approach developed by Sigmund Freud that focuses on uncovering unconscious thoughts and desires to better understand and resolve psychological issues.
2 Psychodynamic therapy is a therapeutic approach rooted in psychoanalysis that emphasizes exploring unconscious processes and past experiences to understand current behaviour and emotional patterns.
3 CBT focuses on identifying and changing negative thought patterns (cognitive distortions) and behaviours that contribute to emotional distress. It emphasizes the relationship between thoughts, feelings, and behaviours.
4 REBT, developed by Albert Ellis, is a more specific form of CBT that focuses on challenging and replacing irrational beliefs with rational ones. It introduces the concept of "ABC" (Activating event, Beliefs, Consequences), emphasizing that it's not the event itself, but the irrational beliefs about the event that lead to emotional distress.

Dialectical Behaviour Therapy (DBT)[1], or Acceptance and Commitment Therapy (ACT)[2], focusing on changing behaviours or alleviating distress. The approaches are more structured and goal-oriented.

For instance, a philosophical counsellor might use Socratic way of questioning to explore a client's conception of success: *"Why do you believe financial success defines your self-worth? What assumptions are you making about failure?"* This kind of dialogue encourages the client to question deeply ingrained beliefs, leading to a more reflective and authentic understanding of their desires.

3. **Philosophical Foundations vs. Psychological Processes:** Philosophical counselling engages with philosophical traditions to resolve existential crises, personal identity conflicts, or ethical dilemmas. It aims for wisdom, self-knowledge, and a coherent worldview. Psychological counselling, in contrast, focuses on psychological processes—like cognition, emotion regulation, and behaviour modification—rooted in the scientific study of the mind and behaviour. Its primary aim is mental health outcomes.

---

1. Dialectical behavioural therapy (DBT) is a type of cognitive-behavioural therapy that emphasizes the development of skills in four key areas: mindfulness, emotional regulation, distress tolerance, and interpersonal effectiveness. Originally developed by Marsha Linehan for treating borderline personality disorder, DBT helps individuals manage intense emotions and improve relationships by balancing acceptance and change.

2. Acceptance and Commitment Therapy (ACT) is a form of psychotherapy that encourages individuals to accept their thoughts and feelings rather than fighting or avoiding them. It focuses on promoting psychological flexibility through mindfulness and behaviour change techniques, helping individuals commit to actions aligned with their core values while reducing the impact of negative thoughts and emotions.

4. **Outcome Orientation:** Philosophical counselling often aims for long-term, abstract outcomes, such as gaining deeper self-knowledge, developing a personal philosophy, or resolving existential dilemmas. Success is measured by the client's ability to live more authentically and in alignment with their values. Psychological counselling typically has more immediate, measurable goals, such as reducing symptoms, improving emotional regulation, and enhancing daily functioning.

5. **Challenges and Intensity:** Philosophical counselling can be intellectually and emotionally demanding. Clients are asked to confront deeply held beliefs, question life choices, and examine the very foundations of their worldview. This process can be unsettling but ultimately transformative. Psychological counselling also involves facing difficult emotions and mental health challenges but is generally more structured to provide immediate relief from distress.

Philosophical Counselling: A Complement to Psychological Healing

Ultimately, both philosophical and psychological counselling offer unique benefits. They do not need to compete—rather, they can go hand in hand. Psychological counselling aids in uncovering the unconscious motivations behind thoughts and behaviours, while philosophical counselling provides a framework for making conscious, value-driven choices. Together, they empower individuals to achieve deeper self-understanding and personal growth.

> **Reflective Exercise: Is Your Crisis Philosophical or Psychological?**
>
> Sometimes, the challenges we face are rooted in psychological difficulties, such as anxiety or depression, while other times they stem from deeper existential or philosophical questions. Use this exercise to reflect on the nature of your current struggle and determine whether philosophical or psychological counselling might be more suitable for you.

Step 1: Self-Reflection on Your Experience

Dedicate 10-15 minutes in a calm, quiet space. Reflect on the nature of your current difficulties. Answer the following questions honestly:

1. **What kind of thoughts are consuming your mind?**

    - Are you constantly ruminating about specific worries, fears, or emotional pain (e.g., feeling anxious about everyday activities or experiencing depressive moods)?

      Psychological Indicators: These are often signs of mental health struggles, like anxiety or depression.

    - Are you questioning the meaning of life, your purpose, or your identity (e.g., asking, *"Why am I here?"* or *"What is my true purpose?"*)?

      Philosophical Indicators: These reflect deeper existential or philosophical concerns.

2. **Are your emotions more intense or deeper than usual?**

    - Do you feel overwhelmingly sad, anxious, or irritable, making it difficult to perform everyday tasks?

Psychological Indicators: Strong emotional reactions that disrupt daily functioning often suggest psychological challenges.

- Do you feel more numb, disillusioned, or disengaged with life, asking if it holds any deeper meaning or purpose?

Philosophical Indicators: These feelings of disconnection often point to existential questions and philosophical struggles.

Step 2: Examine the Source of Your Problem

Reflect on the source of your discomfort. Use these questions as a guide:

1. **Is your difficulty related to mental health?**
   - Are you struggling with patterns of thought, emotion, or behaviour that seem difficult to control (e.g., panic attacks, obsessive thoughts, or prolonged periods of sadness)?

   Psychological Indicator: This suggests you may benefit from psychological Counselling, where symptoms and behavioural patterns are addressed.

2. **Do you find yourself grappling with broader life questions?**
   - Are you wrestling with questions like: *"What is the meaning of my existence? Am I living an authentic life? What is my ethical responsibility in the world?"*

   Philosophical Indicators: These kinds of inquiries are characteristic of philosophical crises, which often benefit from philosophical counselling.

Step 3: Assess Your Goals

Think about what you hope to gain from counselling:

1. **What kind of resolution are you seeking?**
   - Do you want help managing stress, anxiety, or improving your daily functioning?

     Psychological Counselling: This is typically more focused on mental health and well-being.

   - Are you seeking deeper insight into your personal values, life's purpose, or moral dilemmas?

     Philosophical Counselling: This type of counselling offers clarity around your worldview and existential concerns.

Step 4: Reflect on Your Answers

After reflecting on the questions above, consider which side your answers align with more closely:

- If you identified specific emotional or behavioural symptoms (e.g., persistent anxiety, difficulty coping, depression), you may be dealing with a psychological crisis. Psychological counselling, such as psychoanalysis, psychodynamic therapy, Cognitive Behavioural Therapy (CBT) etc. can help address and manage these symptoms.

- If you found yourself grappling with deeper, more abstract questions (e.g., purpose, meaning, identity, values), you may be experiencing a philosophical crisis. Philosophical counselling can help you explore and clarify these existential concerns, guiding you toward wisdom and self-reliance.

Step 5: Final Reflection

Take a few moments to consider:

- Do you feel like your struggles are impacting your mental health and daily functioning, or are they more about finding clarity on life's deeper meaning?

This reflection can guide you toward the type of support you may need. Remember, it's possible to experience both psychological and philosophical struggles at the same time, and seeking help in both areas can be beneficial.

Chapter - 3

Historical and Ancient Roots of Philosophical Counselling

Philosophical counselling, though a contemporary field of practice, has deep roots in both Eastern and Western traditions, where applying philosophical principles to everyday life has always been central. In this chapter, we will explore the Indian and Western philosophical landscapes, both rich with dialogues and teachings that serve as early forms of counselling and guide individuals in their pursuit of wisdom and self-understanding.

Indian Roots of Philosophical Counselling:

Philosophical counselling in India traces its roots to ancient scriptures, where a guru's guidance was essential for personal growth. These ancient texts, like a compass guiding a lost traveller offered direction to those seeking understanding. These texts often feature dialogues between a teacher and a student, resembling the modern practice of philosophical counselling. The *Upanishads*, the *Bhagavad Gita*, and the various systems of Indian philosophy (*Darshanas*) provide some of the most notable examples of this tradition. These ancient dialogues, which explore existential questions, ethical dilemmas, and the challenges of life, laid the foundation for philosophical counselling in India.

The *Upanishads* and Dialogues on the Self:

The *Upanishads*, regarded as the pinnacle of Vedic wisdom, are rich with philosophical dialogues that unfold like a delicate tapestry exploring the nature of reality, the self, and the universe. These dialogues are like windows, opening onto the vast landscape of the mind, offering a clear view of the inner self. For example, in the *Katha Upanishad*, the young seeker Nachiketa engages in a profound dialogue with Yama, the god of death, about the nature of the self and the afterlife. His dialogue embodies the essence of philosophical counselling, guiding the individual toward self-inquiry (*atma vichara*). Just as a determined climber ascends a mountain to glimpse the peak, Nachiketa's dialogue with Yama reveals deeper layers of understanding about life and death. In modern philosophical counselling, a practitioner might similarly guide a client through existential concerns such as the fear of death or the search for self-identity, helping them uncover deeper truths about their existence. The exploration of mortality, much like in the *Katha Upanishad*, can help clients reshape their perspectives on life.

In the *Brihadaranyaka Upanishad*, the dialogue between sage Yajnavalkya and Maitreyi delves into the nature of immortality and the ultimate truth. Yajnavalkya explains that wealth cannot lead to immortality, emphasizing the importance of self-realization and the pursuit of knowledge. Their conversation is like peeling the layers of an onion—each question and answer brings them closer to the core of truth. Similarly, Yajnavalkya's dialogue with

Gargi addresses the nature of reality and the essence of the universe. These discussions reveal the limitations of human understanding and stress the importance of realizing the underlying unity of existence. In today's philosophical counselling, these ancient discussions on material wealth, immortality, and the nature of reality are mirrored in conversations about meaning, value, and human fulfilment. Clients might explore what truly brings them happiness and whether external achievements align with their deeper existential needs.

The *Bhagavad Gita*: Ethical Dilemmas and Self-Realization:

Another significant example of early philosophical counselling is found in the *Bhagavad Gita*, where Lord Krishna counsels the warrior Arjuna on the battlefield of Kurukshetra. Overwhelmed by the moral dilemma of fighting his own kin, Arjuna seeks guidance from Krishna. Through their dialogue, Krishna provides Arjuna with a deeper understanding of duty, righteousness, and the nature of the self, ultimately guiding him toward a path of enlightened action. Krishna's words are like a beacon in a storm, providing Arjuna with clarity amid his turmoil. This dialogue serves as a powerful example of philosophical counselling, addressing questions of *ethics, identity, and purpose*. In philosophical counselling, moral dilemmas similar to Arjuna's—whether concerning personal ethics or difficult life choices—are a common focus. Modern clients may face complex ethical decisions, and the role of the counsellor is to help them navigate these dilemmas by understanding their values and duties, just as Krishna guides Arjuna through his internal conflict.

The *Ashtavakra Gita* and Dialogues on Self-Liberation:

The *Ashtavakra Gita* presents another important dialogue, this time between the sage Ashtavakra[1] and King Janaka. In this text, Ashtavakra offers guidance on self-liberation and the realization of the self as pure consciousness, beyond the constraints of the physical world. This dialogue exemplifies philosophical counselling, as the sage helps the king let go of worldly attachments and find inner peace and wisdom.

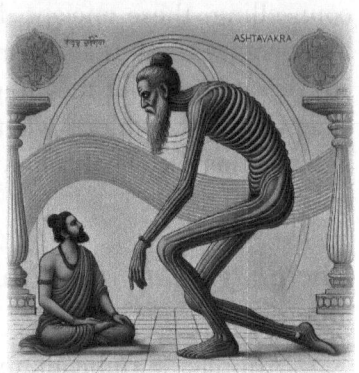

Ashtavakra's teachings are like a river, gently washing away the illusions of the physical world, leaving behind only the purity of the self. Today, philosophical counselling often helps individuals who feel trapped by their materialistic pursuits or societal pressures. Through reflective dialogue, counsellors guide clients in understanding their deeper, non-material selves and discovering the freedom that comes from self-awareness and inner peace. This mirrors the ancient guidance Ashtavakra provided to King Janaka.

Buddhist Dialogues: Exploring the Self and Consciousness:

In addition to the *Upanishads* and the *Bhagavad Gita*, Buddhist philosophical texts such as the *Milinda-*

---

1 Ashtavakra was a sage from ancient Indian tradition, known for his wisdom despite being physically deformed from birth, hence the name "Ashtavakra", meaning "eight bends" in Sanskrit. He is best known for his dialogue with King Janaka in the *Ashtavakra Gita*.

Panha¹ also present dialogues that reflect early forms of counselling. In this text, King Milinda engages in a dialogue with the Buddhist sage Nagasena about identity, consciousness, and the nature of reality. Much like in the *Milinda-Panha*, philosophical counsellors today help clients disentangle complex questions about identity and reality. Clients often explore who they are beyond their societal roles, and the counsellor, like Nagasena, helps them work through these layers, guiding them toward greater clarity. These conversations, like their Hindu counterparts, were not just theoretical—they were intended to transform the individual's understanding and approach to life. In modern philosophical counselling, these principles live on. Counsellors help clients apply these ancient questions to their contemporary struggles, transforming their approach to life's challenges. In this way, they laid the foundation for what we now recognize as philosophical counselling, a practice that continues to evolve and adapt in modern contexts.

Western Roots of Philosophical Counselling

The idea that philosophy is a practical tool for living dates back to Socrates. In ancient Greece, Socrates practiced an early form of philosophical counselling in the Athenian marketplace, using dialogue to help people understand themselves and live examined lives. Today's philosophical counsellors continue Socratic dialogue, guiding clients through self-examination by asking probing questions, much like Socrates did. The counsellor doesn't impose

---

1 The *Milinda Panha* (Questions of King Milinda) is a significant Buddhist text composed as a dialogue between the Indo-Greek King Milinda (also known as Menander) and the Buddhist sage Nagasena. The *Milinda Panha* is valued for its clear and engaging presentation of complex Buddhist ideas.

answers but helps the individual arrive at deeper truths through dialogue, making the process more about personal discovery than instruction.

Socratic Dialogue: The Foundation of Western Philosophical Counselling

Socrates' method, now known as Socratic dialogue, encouraged deep questioning and self-examination. He believed that by asking the right questions, individuals could "give birth" to their own wisdom—in many ways, this Socratic method of questioning still forms the backbone of modern philosophical counselling, where clients are guided to discover their own wisdom through critical thinking and self-reflection.

Hellenistic Schools: Stoicism and Epicureanism as Philosophical Practices

This practical application of philosophy continued through the Hellenistic period, with schools like the Stoics and Epicureans, who emphasized philosophy as a way of life. These philosophers, through what Pierre Hadot[1] describes as "spiritual exercises", sought to cultivate inner virtue and tranquillity by applying philosophical principles to everyday life. To them, philosophy wasn't an intellectual pursuit—it was like a daily workout for the soul, building resilience and wisdom through constant practice. Modern philosophical counselling often incorporates these Hellenistic ideas. In contemporary practice, the Stoic emphasis on focusing

---

1 Pierre Hadot was a French philosopher and historian, best known for his work on ancient philosophy. His influential works, such as *Philosophy as a Way of Life* and *What is Ancient Philosophy?* emphasize that philosophy in antiquity was a set of spiritual exercises designed to guide individuals toward wisdom, virtue, and inner freedom.

only on what is within our control can help clients dealing with anxiety or uncertainty, while the Epicurean pursuit of simple pleasures mirrors modern discussions about living a balanced, mindful life.

Modern Foundations:

In the modern era, Dr. Pierre Grimes[1] laid further foundations for philosophical counselling by establishing The Noetic Society in 1967. His work focused on dialogue and dialectic, leading to the creation of the "Philosophical Midwifery Program" in 1978. This idea of "midwifery" is reflected in modern philosophical counselling, where the counsellor doesn't give direct answers but helps the client discover their own truths through dialogue. This approach is like a skilled midwife aiding in the delivery of wisdom that already resides within the person, waiting to emerge.

A pivotal moment for philosophical counselling came in 1981 when Gerd Achenbach in Germany pioneered what became known as "Philosophical Practice". In 1982, the "Society for Philosophical Practice" was founded in Germany, which later became the "International Society for Philosophical Practice", serving as the umbrella organization for various national societies. These modern developments have brought philosophical counselling into the professional realm, where counsellors are trained to use ancient wisdom as a tool for addressing contemporary existential and ethical dilemmas. Achenbach's groundbreaking work was quickly followed by other notable practitioners like Ad Hoogendijk, Ida Jongsma, Will Heutz, and Dries Boele in Holland, as well as Shlomit Schuster in Israel. The movement gained momentum, and in 1994, practical philosophers from around

---

[1] Dr. Pierre Grimes is an American philosopher and a prominent figure in the field of philosophical counselling.

the globe convened at the First International Conference in Canada, co-organized by Ran Lahav and Lou Marinoff. This event was crucial in popularizing philosophical counselling in the English-speaking world.

Conclusion

From the ancient dialogues of the *Upanishads* to the philosophical midwifery of Socrates, philosophical counselling has a long history of guiding individuals toward greater self-understanding and wisdom. These foundational practices were not merely abstract conversations; they were deeply practical tools aimed at transforming the individual's life. Just as Yajnavalkya helped Maitreyi question the value of material wealth in the pursuit of immortality, or Socrates challenged Athenians to think critically about justice, these dialogues addressed the fundamental concerns of human existence—questions that are just as relevant today as they were thousands of years ago.

These ancient roots continue to influence modern philosophical counselling practices, offering timeless frameworks for addressing life's existential and ethical challenges. The focus on self-inquiry, ethical reflection, and personal growth forms the backbone of contemporary philosophical counselling, where the goal is not just to resolve mental health issues but to explore the deeper meanings behind our thoughts, actions, and values.

As we move forward into the next chapter, we will explore the approaches and methods of modern philosophical counselling, seeing how these ancient roots have evolved into a structured practice that guides individuals through their most profound questions about existence, meaning, value and purpose.

> **Reflective Exercise:**
>
> In ancient traditions like the *Upanishads*, the *Bhagavad Gita*, and Socratic dialogues, dialectical methods were used to probe the most profound truths about self, consciousness, death, and ethics. This exercise invites you to step into the role of both questioner and responder, engaging in a personal dialogue that mirrors the ancient method of philosophical inquiry. Your goal is not to find immediate answers, but to explore and challenge your deepest assumptions about life's most pressing questions.

Step 1: Choose Your Philosophical Focus

Begin by selecting one of the following themes that resonate most with you. This will be the foundation of your inquiry:

1. The nature of the *self* (Who am I beyond the roles and labels that define me?)
2. The concept of *death* (How does my understanding of death shape my approach to life?)
3. *Consciousness* (What is the source of my awareness, and how do I experience it?)
4. *Ethics* (What principles guide my moral choices, and why do I hold them?)

Step 2: Engage in Deep, Probing Questions

Enter into a dialogue with yourself, much like the ancient sages and philosophers did. Each question you ask should lead you deeper into reflection. Challenge every answer—just as Socrates would in the Athenian marketplace or a guru might in an *Upanishadic* discourse. Avoid settling for surface responses; continue digging.

- **For Self:**
    - What defines me? Is it my profession, relationships, or achievements?

- o If I strip away these external labels, what remains at the core of who I am?
- o Is there a constant "self", or is my identity fluid and ever-changing?

- **For Death:**
  - o What do I truly fear about death?
  - o How does my understanding of death influence the way I live each day?
  - o If I were to accept death as a natural part of life, how might that shift my choices and priorities?

- **For Consciousness:**
  - o Where does my awareness originate?
  - o Am I the creator of my thoughts, or simply the observer of them?
  - o Can my consciousness exist beyond the physical body, or is it bound to it?

- **For Ethics:**
  - o What motivates my sense of right and wrong?
  - o Are my moral values shaped by society, family, or are they internally derived?
  - o How do these ethical principles guide me when I face difficult decisions?

Step 3: Challenge the Assumptions Behind Your Responses

After answering each question, pause and reflect: are your answers grounded in societal conditioning, personal experience, or deeper wisdom? Challenge your own assumptions and look for inconsistencies.

For example:

- If you believe your identity is tied to your job, ask: *What happens to my sense of self if I lose that job?*

Does my value diminish, or is there something more enduring?
- If you fear death, explore: *Is it the unknown that frightens me, or the finality of it? Why do I fear what I don't fully understand?*

Step 4: Consider Ancient Perspectives

Reflect on how great philosophical figures might have responded to these same questions. Incorporating their wisdom can deepen your understanding:

- Socrates famously said, "The unexamined life is not worth living." How does this influence your exploration of the self?
- In the *Bhagavad Gita*, Krishna advises detachment from the ego and outcomes. How might letting go of attachment help you live with more purpose and clarity?
- In the *Katha Upanishad*, Nachiketa learns from Yama, the god of death, that death is not an end to be feared but a passage to deeper understanding. How does this perspective shift your view of mortality?

Step 5: Record Your Insights

As you conclude this internal dialogue, write down any new insights, realizations, or shifts in perspective. How has your understanding of self, death, consciousness, or ethics evolved through this process? What, if anything, feels clearer or resolved?

Goal:

This exercise is not about arriving at definitive answers. Like the ancient dialogues, its purpose is to cultivate deeper inquiry and self-awareness. Through repeated reflection, you may find that clarity and insight come not from having all the answers, but from learning to ask the right questions. In time, this habit of introspective questioning can lead to greater wisdom, purpose, and peace in how you live and make decisions.

Chapter - 4

Fundamental Approaches and Methods in Philosophical Counselling

Philosophical counselling offers a wide array of approaches, each uniquely designed to address the diverse challenges we face in life. But how do we choose the right path? Whether you're seeking clarity on moral dilemmas, exploring your sense of purpose, or untangling complex emotional conflicts, the approach your counsellor takes can make all the difference.

In this chapter, we'll explore the core philosophical frameworks that guide counselling sessions, each serving as a compass for piloting personal growth, self-reflection, and decision-making.

The Critical Thinking Approach

The Critical Thinking Approach is centred around the art of reasoning and employs a range of thinking tools to address personal problems. This approach involves techniques such as formulating arguments, detecting logical fallacies, analysing concepts, and exposing hidden assumptions. Simply put, it's about teaching clients to think more clearly and logically. For instance, if someone feels anxious about an upcoming event, they might assume that failure will lead to shame. By guiding them to logically challenge that assumption through evidence, they can realize that their fears may be exaggerated or unfounded. By employing these critical thinking tools, counsellors aim to help clients analyse their beliefs, behaviours, and emotions. It is especially useful for clients dealing with specific, well-defined issues  like anxiety, relationship stress, or workplace challenges. By encouraging clients to break down and critically assess their thought processes, this method helps them resolve concrete problems and regain a sense of control over their lives.

Best for: Clients seeking practical, structured solutions to well-defined personal issues, such as managing stress, decision-making, or emotional regulation.

Case Example:

Client: Sarah, a mid-level manager, has been experiencing severe anxiety about an upcoming presentation to senior executives. She fears that one small mistake during the presentation will completely undermine her professional reputation.

Counselling: The counsellor helps Sarah deconstruct this belief using critical thinking techniques. They begin by identifying Sarah's underlying assumption: "If I make a mistake, I will lose all credibility." Through a series of probing questions, Sarah is encouraged to examine this belief logically: *Is it reasonable to think that one mistake will destroy her reputation? Is there evidence to support that senior executives are so unforgiving?* Together, they identify the logical fallacy of "catastrophizing"[1] in Sarah's thinking. The counsellor guides Sarah to reframe her belief: "Making a small mistake is natural, and it doesn't define my competence or worth." This new, balanced perspective helps Sarah manage her anxiety and approach the presentation with confidence.

The Edification Approach

The Edification Approach views philosophical counselling as a personal journey towards greater wisdom and meaning rather than a process to solve specific problems. In simpler terms, it's about seeing life as a continuous learning experience. It works best for clients seeking deeper self-understanding and personal growth, especially those who are not necessarily focused on resolving immediate issues like workplace stress but are instead looking to reflect on their values and life purpose. A client may come in to discuss a specific issue, but this approach encourages them to explore larger questions like, *"What do I really value?"* or *"How can I live more meaningfully?"* This reflective process can inspire new ways of understanding themselves and their world. It encourages clients to reflect deeply on their values and beliefs and to engage with transformative ideas that inspire personal growth. The aim is not merely to resolve issues but to enrich the client's understanding of their world, fostering ongoing self-discovery and meaning-making.

Best for: Clients on a path of self-discovery or those looking for philosophical enrichment, where the journey is more important than arriving at a specific solution.

---

1 Catastrophizing is a cognitive distortion and a logical fallacy where a person assumes the worst possible outcome in a situation, often without sufficient evidence. This fallacy involves irrationally exaggerating the severity or likelihood of negative events, leading to heightened anxiety and fear.

Case Example:

Client: Ravi, a 45-year-old executive, feels increasingly disillusioned with his career despite years of success. He finds himself questioning the meaning of his work and the direction of his life.

Counselling: Rather than offering solutions to Ravi's dissatisfaction, the counsellor invites him into a reflective journey, exploring deeper questions about purpose and fulfilment. Together, they examine Ravi's long-held beliefs about success, personal worth, and external validation. Over time, Ravi realizes that his pursuit of career achievement has been driven more by societal expectations than by his personal values. Through ongoing philosophical exploration, Ravi reconnects with a passion for mentoring and community service, which had been sidelined in favour of professional advancement. This reflective process leads Ravi to redefine his understanding of success, shifting from external achievements to personal growth and meaningful connections.

The Casuistical Method

The casuistical method addresses moral dilemmas by comparing the client's current problem to other ethical situations. This is essentially a way to analyse ethical issues by drawing parallels to similar cases. Think of it as a way to figure out tough moral questions by looking at how similar situations were handled. This approach is most suitable for clients facing ethical or moral dilemmas where clear-cut answers may not exist. For example, if someone is struggling with a personal ethical question, like whether to tell the truth in a difficult situation, the counsellor might help them compare this to other moral dilemmas to find clarity. Or if a client is uncertain about the morality of abortion, the counsellor may discuss similar dilemmas, such as euthanasia or the moral justification for war, to provide a broader context. These scenarios help the client understand the nuanced nature of ethical principles and clarify their own ethical stance. The goal is to assist clients in understanding and articulating their own beliefs about right and wrong, rather than providing prescriptive answers.

Best for: Clients dealing with complex moral dilemmas and seeking a structured exploration of ethical principles through analogy.

Case Example:

Client: Dr. Maya, a paediatrician, is faced with a difficult decision regarding a severely ill newborn whose parents refuse life-saving surgery due to their religious beliefs.

Counselling: Dr. Maya feels torn between her duty to protect the child's life and the parents' right to make decisions based on their religious convictions. In counselling, the practitioner presents similar ethical dilemmas, such as cases where doctors are faced with refusing blood transfusions for children because of religious beliefs or cases of parental refusal of vaccinations. By comparing these situations, Dr. Maya is guided to reflect on the ethical principles of beneficence (acting in the best interest of the child), autonomy (respecting the parents' wishes), and justice (considering the child's right to life and future autonomy). Through this process, Dr. Maya recognizes that while respecting religious beliefs is critical, her ethical obligation to the child as a vulnerable patient must take precedence. She ultimately decides to pursue legal intervention to ensure the child receives the necessary surgery, concluding that her professional duty to safeguard the child's life is paramount in this case.

The Contractarian Approach

The Contractarian Approach is based on the idea of forming agreements or "contracts" between individuals, similar to how societies set up social contracts. In philosophical counselling, this means helping clients make decisions based on their own values by imagining they are creating a contract with themselves. It is particularly helpful for clients looking to align their decisions with their ethical framework, especially in situations involving fairness, justice, or personal integrity. By exploring hypothetical contracts, clients can examine their values and make decisions that reflect their own beliefs. For example, if someone is deciding how to handle a personal conflict, the counsellor might ask, *"What would a fair agreement between your needs and the other person's look like?"* This approach guides clients in aligning their choices with their personal values and ethics, encouraging deeper understanding of how they negotiate decisions.

Best for: Clients who are focused on ethical decision-making or aligning their actions with their personal value system, especially in conflicts of fairness or justice.

Case Example:

Client: Jason, a tech entrepreneur, faces an ethical dilemma: he is offered a partnership deal that could rapidly expand his company but requires him to overlook questionable data privacy practices.

Counselling: To help Jason evaluate the decision, the counsellor guides him through a hypothetical contract exercise. Jason is asked to imagine a scenario where he is drafting a fair contract not just for himself but for all stakeholders, including customers, employees, and society. Through this thought experiment, Jason realizes that compromising on privacy undermines the ethical foundation of his company, which prides itself on transparency and trust. By reflecting on his personal and professional values, Jason concludes that maintaining his ethical standards, even at the cost of rapid growth, is the right choice. He rejects the deal, confident that his decision aligns with his long-term vision and the ethical principles upon which his company was built.

Core Methods in Philosophical Counselling

Philosophical Counselling methods, on the other hand, refer to the specific techniques or procedures used within an approach. These methods are not rigid formulas but adaptable approaches that shape the dialogue. Each method offers a distinct pathway tailored to the unique concerns of the individual, whether they seek insight into life's meaning or relief from irrational beliefs.

Directive vs. Non-Directive Methods in Philosophical Counselling

Philosophical counselling offers both directive and non-directive methods, each with distinct advantages depending on the client's needs and the nature of their concerns.

- **Non-Directive Methods**: Non-directive methods, such as Achenbach's Open-Ended Method or the Socratic Method, emphasize open exploration and self-discovery. These approaches are client-centred, allowing the counselee to articulate their thoughts and feelings without immediate intervention or judgment from the counsellor. The aim is to create a supportive, reflective space where clients can arrive at their own insights through guided conversation.

Advantages:
- o Ideal for clients dealing with abstract or existential issues, such as "What is the purpose of my life?" or "Who am I beyond my societal roles?"
- o Encourages deep self-reflection, allowing clients to engage in an ongoing process of self-inquiry.
- o Particularly useful for individuals who are in search of meaning or wish to explore different perspectives without seeking a quick resolution.
- o **Best suited for**: Clients who are already self-motivated, comfortable with introspection, and not seeking immediate answers, but rather the space to explore complex ideas at their own pace.

- **Directive Methods**: Directive approaches, such as Logic-Based Therapy (LBT) or Philosophical Midwifery, offer more structure and guidance. These methods involve a more active role for the counsellor, who works to directly challenge irrational beliefs or help clients reframe unhelpful assumptions. In these approaches, the counsellor takes the lead in steering the conversation toward specific solutions or insights.

Advantages:
- o Effective for clients struggling with immediate cognitive or emotional challenges, such as irrational fears, anxiety, or unexamined beliefs.
- o Provides clearer, more concrete steps toward resolving issues, such as helping the client restructure harmful thought patterns or uncover subconscious beliefs.
- o **Best suited for**: Clients who need more focused guidance, perhaps due to distress caused by particular irrational beliefs or emotional difficulties.

It's also appropriate for those seeking actionable steps or resolutions rather than broad philosophical exploration.

Gerd Achenbach's Open-Ended Method:

Have you ever found that structured advice doesn't quite fit your unique life situation? Or have you ever felt overwhelmed by the complexity of a problem, unsure where to begin? The Open-Ended Method allows the conversation to evolve naturally, helping you uncover layers of your experience and see your situation from new angles. Gerd Achenbach's method is characterized by its adaptability and open-ended nature. Rather than following a strict, predefined structure, the counsellor engages with the counselee in a flexible manner, allowing the dialogue to evolve based on the specific issues presented. The focus is on cultivating deep self-reflection and personal growth, as the counsellor guides the individual to broaden their perspectives and explore the root causes of their concerns. For example, a client struggling with the meaning of success might begin the conversation by expressing dissatisfaction with their career trajectory. Through open-ended questioning, the counsellor could lead the client to uncover deeper concerns about self-worth or societal expectations that were previously unacknowledged. The dialogue unfolds naturally, allowing the client to explore these insights at their own pace. The counsellor acts as a guide rather than a prescriber of solutions, encouraging a process of discovery rather than providing concrete answers.

Socratic Method:

Do you ever find yourself accepting assumptions without questioning them? The Socratic method helps you critically examine your beliefs to uncover deeper truths.

The Socratic method is a structured dialogical approach that encourages critical thinking and self-examination. The counsellor engages the counselee through open-ended questions designed to uncover assumptions, challenge inconsistencies, and clarify beliefs. This method helps the counselee explore their thoughts and beliefs more deeply, fostering an understanding of underlying assumptions that shape their worldview. For instance, a client questioning their happiness might initially state that wealth is his source of satisfaction. The Socratic method would involve the counsellor asking probing questions like, *"What does happiness mean to you?"* or *"Is wealth the only pathway to fulfilment?"* Through such inquiry, the client begins to realize that their assumptions about happiness are more complex and perhaps influenced by external pressures. The aim is to foster critical thinking skills that the counselee can apply to their life challenges, promoting clarity and coherence in their belief system.

Logic-Based Therapy (LBT):

Have you ever felt that a single irrational thought was driving much of your stress? How would your life change if you could challenge and replace that thought? Logic-Based Therapy (LBT), developed by Elliot D. Cohen, is an approach that focuses on identifying and challenging irrational beliefs. These beliefs are often the root cause of emotional distress and problematic behaviours. The counsellor works with the counselee to identify these irrational thoughts, analyse them logically, and replace them with more rational alternatives.

LBT emphasizes the importance of personal responsibility and cognitive restructuring, helping counselees develop healthier and more constructive thought patterns. For example, a client may struggle with the belief that "I must be perfect to be loved". Using LBT, the counsellor would help the client analyse this belief, revealing that perfection is unattainable and unnecessary for meaningful relationships. By restructuring this irrational thought into something more rational, such as "I am worthy of love despite my imperfections", the client can begin to shift their emotional responses and behaviours accordingly.

Logotherapy:

Do you ever feel a void, as though your life lacks meaning or purpose? What if the meaning you seek is something you can create? Logotherapy helps you explore your sense of purpose and find meaning even in the most difficult circumstances. Logotherapy, founded by Viktor Frankl, is an existential therapeutic approach that emphasizes the search for meaning in life. This method is particularly suited for individuals who feel a lack of purpose or are struggling with existential crises. The counsellor helps the counselee explore deep questions of purpose, values, and meaning, encouraging them to find or create a sense of meaning in their lives. For instance, a client might express feelings of emptiness and despair, wondering what the purpose of their life is. The counsellor, using Logotherapy, might ask, *"What makes life worth living for you?"* or *"Can meaning emerge from suffering?"* By guiding the client to reflect on these existential questions, the counsellor helps them uncover values that resonate with their sense of self, whether that be through personal growth, relationships, or contributing to something larger than themselves. Techniques in logotherapy often involve discussions around the "will to meaning" and addressing feelings of emptiness or the "existential vacuum".

Philosophical Midwifery:

Are there hidden beliefs or assumptions holding you back, buried deep in your subconscious? What might you discover if you could bring these hidden thoughts into the light? Philosophical Midwifery helps you unearth those underlying thoughts and reshape them. Philosophical Midwifery, inspired by Socratic maieutics and developed by Pierre Grimes, involves guiding the counselee through self-discovery by uncovering unconscious beliefs and assumptions. Often, this method incorporates dream analysis as a way to bring hidden thoughts to light.

The counsellor acts as a "midwife" to the counselee's thoughts, helping them critically examine and reframe deeply held beliefs that may be causing distress. For example, a client might experience recurring dreams about failure, which reflect unconscious fears about their professional life. By analysing the symbolism of the dreams and connecting them to the client's waking concerns, the counsellor helps bring these hidden beliefs into consciousness, allowing the client to challenge and reshape them. This approach encourages profound introspection and the reformation of one's worldview.

Phenomenological Analysis:

How do your personal experiences shape your

perception of reality? Phenomenological analysis helps you uncover the ways your unique experiences influence how you understand the world. Phenomenological analysis is based on the philosophical tradition of phenomenology, which emphasizes the direct exploration of experience. The counsellor encourages the counselee to describe their experiences in detail, focusing on how they perceive and interpret the world around them. This method seeks to uncover patterns in the counselee's subjective experience, offering insights into how their perceptions shape their understanding of reality. For example, a client may describe a sense of isolation or alienation in their daily interactions. The counsellor might ask them to describe specific moments when these feelings arise—how the client perceives others, their own emotions, and how they react to situations. By exploring the nuances of these experiences, the counsellor helps the client gain awareness of the subjective lens through which they view the world, revealing how certain patterns of perception contribute to their emotional state. The goal is to provide the client with a deeper awareness of their lived experience, allowing them to reframe their understanding of social dynamics and personal relationships.

Existential Dialogue:

Do you find yourself questioning the fundamental aspects of your existence—freedom, responsibility, and authenticity? Existential dialogue helps you confront these deep concerns and find your path forward. Existential dialogue is an approach grounded in existential philosophy, focusing on the fundamental questions of existence, freedom, responsibility, and authenticity. The counsellor engages the counselee in deep, reflective conversations about their existential concerns, such as the search for meaning, the confrontation with mortality, and the challenge of making authentic choices. For instance, a client might express anxiety about the direction of their life. The counsellor may ask reflective questions like, *"What would it mean for you to live an authentic life?"* or *"How do you understand your freedom to make choices?"* These questions invite the client to engage deeply with their existential anxieties and, in doing so, discover paths toward greater self-awareness and authenticity. This method helps the counselee navigate existential anxiety and develop a more authentic approach to living, encouraging them to embrace the freedom and responsibility inherent in their existence.

Conclusion:

Philosophical counselling is a diverse field that offers both flexibility and depth, allowing each session to be tailored to the unique needs and goals of the individual. Whether the counsellor takes a non-directive or directive approach, the methods used in philosophical counselling serve as powerful tools to help the counselee manage life's most complex challenges. From guiding a client through deep existential crises to helping them reframe irrational beliefs, the goal remains the same—to foster clarity, growth, and self-understanding.

One of the strengths of philosophical counselling is its adaptability. Different methods can be applied depending on the situation and the individual's readiness for self-exploration or problem-solving. The beauty of this flexibility is that philosophical counselling does not adhere to a one-size-fits-all model; it evolves with the client, adapting to their changing needs as they grow through the process.

At its core, philosophical counselling is about empowerment — empowering individuals to question, to reflect, and ultimately to take responsibility for their own philosophical journey. The methods are not simply tools to resolve a crisis but instruments for lifelong inquiry. Through ongoing self-reflection and critical thinking, clients can continue to apply the principles they've learned in counselling long after the sessions have ended, making philosophy an integral part of their daily lives.

In the chapters ahead, we will continue to explore how these philosophical practices can be applied to real-life scenarios, offering practical guidance for those seeking clarity, meaning, and direction. Remember, the journey of philosophical inquiry is not one of destination but of transformation. The tools and methods presented here are meant to be revisited, refined, and reapplied as you continue to grow and change.

Chapter - 5

Key Stages of Philosophical Counselling

Philosophical counselling is not a rigid process but a fluid journey of exploration and understanding. Each stage serves as a stepping stone, guiding the counselee from initial concerns to the development of a well-formed personal philosophy. At the heart of this journey is the collaborative dialogue between counsellor and counselee, where deep reflection, questioning, and analysis take place. Through these stages, the counselee begins to dismantle old assumptions, challenge ingrained beliefs, and construct a clearer, more authentic view of their life. Together, counsellor and counselee navigate this transformative process, equipping the counselee with tools for lifelong philosophical inquiry and personal growth.

Analytical Stage:

The counselling process begins with the analytical stage, where the counsellor establishes a rapport with the counselee to create a safe space for dialogue. The primary goal is to assess the counselee's needs, concerns, and objectives. By listening to the counselee's story, the counsellor identifies key issues and evaluates whether philosophical counselling is appropriate. The counsellor also determines if any issues require referral to other professionals. During this stage, problematic beliefs, conceptual confusion, and psychological factors that may hinder critical reasoning are identified and explored. Once a solid understanding of the counselee's concerns is achieved, the process moves to the next stage, where deeper philosophical inquiry takes place.

Example prompts for this stage:
- "Can you describe what has led you to seek philosophical counselling at this point in your life?"
- "What thoughts or events have been weighing heavily on your mind recently?"

Counselee's active role:
- The counselee is encouraged to reflect on and articulate their motivations for seeking help, fostering self-awareness from the outset.
- They actively consider how their beliefs and emotions are interconnected, participating in defining the key issues they wish to address.

Synthetic Stage:
In the synthetic stage, the counsellor delves deeper into the counselee's concerns through philosophical dialogue. The focus is on uncovering and articulating the philosophical themes underlying the counselee's issues, such as beliefs about the self, life's purpose, and values. This stage helps the counselee clarify their worldview and develop a coherent perspective on their life situation.

Example prompts for this stage:
- "When you think about this challenge, what personal beliefs come to the surface?"

- "How do you see these experiences shaping your understanding of who you are or where you're heading in life?"

Counselee's role:

- The counselee examines their beliefs, identifying how they relate to their experiences and sense of self.
- They are actively involved in connecting philosophical themes to their own life journey.

Critical Stage:

The critical stage is characterized by a reflective examination of the counselee's beliefs and values. The counsellor employs Socratic questioning to challenge any inconsistencies, irrational beliefs, or conceptual confusion. This stage is crucial for helping the counselee achieve greater clarity and understanding of how their beliefs influence their emotions, behaviours, and relationships. Philosophical tools are introduced to aid in the analysis and critique of fundamental assumptions.

Example prompts for this stage:

- "What happens if we examine this belief from a different angle—does it still hold up?"
- "Can you identify any inconsistencies between what you believe and how you act on those beliefs?"
- "If this assumption were removed, how would that alter your perspective on the problem?"

Counselee's role:

- The counselee engages deeply in questioning their own assumptions and beliefs.

- They critically assess how these beliefs influence their emotions, actions, and relationships.

Comparative Stage:

In the comparative stage, the counselee is encouraged to evaluate their personal philosophy in light of various philosophical theories and concepts. The counsellor presents relevant philosophical ideas that offer new insights or alternative viewpoints. This comparative analysis allows the counselee to critically assess their beliefs and values, fostering a deeper and more nuanced understanding of their life philosophy.

Example prompts for this stage:
- "Have you come across any philosophical teachings that resonate with what you're experiencing?"
- "Let's explore how the concept of 'freedom' in existentialism compares with your views—does it change how you approach this challenge?"

Counselee's role:
- The counselee reflects on their personal beliefs and compares them with ideas from different philosophical traditions.
- They assess how these new perspectives might challenge or enrich their worldview.

Development of Personal Philosophy:

Building on the insights gained, this stage focuses on helping the counselee develop or refine their personal philosophy. The counsellor guides the counselee in integrating these philosophical insights into their daily life, ensuring they are practical and applicable. The aim is for the counselee to create a guiding framework that supports them in navigating life's challenges.

Example prompts for this stage:
- "Having examined these insights, let's consider how can they help shape your approach to future challenges?"
- "How can this newfound clarity inform your decisions moving forward, ensuring they align with your core values?"

Counselee's role:
- The counselee shapes their personal philosophy, integrating new insights into their daily life.
- They begin to align their actions and decisions with the philosophical values they have clarified.

Reflection on Progress and Closure:

The final stage involves reflecting on the progress made during the counselling process. Counsellor and counselee review the insights and changes that have occurred, assessing their impact on the counselee's life. This stage also marks the conclusion of the counselling relationship, with the counsellor encouraging the counselee to continue their philosophical exploration independently, empowering them to maintain and expand their understanding beyond the sessions.

Example prompts for this stage:
- "Reflecting on our journey together, what has been the most significant shift in your thinking?"
- "What steps will you take to ensure that this philosophical inquiry remains an ongoing part of your life?"

- "As you move forward, what new philosophical questions will you continue to explore on your own?"

Counselee's role:
- The counselee reviews their growth, reflecting on key philosophical shifts and new understandings.
- They commit to continuing their philosophical journey beyond the sessions.

Case Example: Handling Social Anxiety in The Digital Age:

Client Background: Jessica, a 22-year-old student, is struggling with severe social anxiety, exacerbated by her constant exposure to social media. She feels overwhelmed by the need to present a perfect image online, comparing herself to others and feeling inadequate. Her fear of judgment and rejection keeps her from authentic interactions in both digital and real-world environments.

- **Analytical Stage:** Jessica opens up about her fear of rejection and the pressure she feels to maintain a perfect online presence. The counsellor identifies that her struggle is rooted in deeper philosophical concerns about identity, self-worth, and the nature of authenticity.
- **Synthetic Stage:** The counsellor helps Jessica explore how social media affects her sense of self. Through guided dialogue, Jessica realizes that she's been living

according to external validation rather than her own values, and she begins questioning her need for approval from others.

- **Critical Stage:** The counsellor challenges Jessica's belief that her worth is tied to her digital persona. Through questioning, Jessica begins to critically examine how much of her self-esteem is based on an idealized version of herself that she feels pressured to maintain.

- **Comparative Stage:** Jessica explores concepts of authenticity and self-identity from existentialist and Buddhist perspectives, learning that the self is fluid and that embracing imperfections can lead to a more authentic existence. She also considers the Stoic idea of focusing on what she can control—her own actions and thoughts, rather than the opinions of others.

- **Development of Personal Philosophy:** Jessica starts to embrace the idea that her self-worth doesn't depend on external approval. She adopts a personal philosophy of authenticity, committing to engage in online and offline spaces in ways that reflect her true self, rather than a curated version for others.

- **Reflection on Progress and Closure:** By the end of counselling, Jessica reflects on her new understanding of self-worth. She feels more grounded in her identity and less swayed by the pressures of social comparison, prepared to approach social interactions with more confidence and authenticity.

In the case of Jessica's struggle with social anxiety, we see how philosophical counselling can offer an approach that goes beyond immediate coping mechanisms. By guiding Jessica through a process of self-exploration and philosophical reflection, the counsellor helps her uncover

the deeper existential and ethical questions behind her anxiety—such as authenticity, self-worth, and the influence of social media on identity. Through this structured process, Jessica is empowered to reshape her understanding of herself, moving away from external validation and toward a more authentic and grounded sense of being. Thus, philosophical counselling provides a framework for individuals facing various modern-day challenges.

While the stages of philosophical counselling provide a structured framework for addressing personal challenges, the effectiveness of these stages often depends on the philosophical traditions and methods that guide the dialogue. In particular, Indian philosophy offers a wealth of insights and practices that can enhance the counselling process. In the following chapter, we will explore the key methods and practices in Indian philosophy, uncovering how these ancient wisdom traditions can inform and deepen the practice of philosophical counselling today.

Chapter - 6

Exploring Methods and Practices in Indian Philosophy

In this chapter, we delve into a selection of profound philosophical, existential, and ethical questions that individuals universally encounter at different points in life. These questions often centre on the nature of suffering, personal growth, the relationship between oneself and the world, and the search for self-identity. To deal with these fundamental issues, we will explore how Indian philosophical traditions provide meaningful insights and practical tools for reflection and growth.

India's philosophical landscape is vast, with a wealth of teachings that address nearly every facet of human experience. For the purposes of this chapter, we've intentionally focused on a curated set of concepts—those that are particularly relevant and impactful for addressing today's core existential concerns. This selection allows us to offer practical applications of these timeless ideas without overwhelming the reader with the breadth of the entire tradition.

Furthermore, the absence of a formal regulatory body for philosophical counselling in India opens a unique space for experimentation. This flexibility allows for the adaptation of these philosophical methods to meet individual needs, creating personalised paths for self-discovery and existential clarity.

In the following sections, we will test these philosophical tools through hypothetical counselling sessions, making the theories accessible and relatable. These thought experiments will showcase how ancient wisdom can guide modern lives toward greater self-awareness and meaning.

Introduction to the *Neti Neti* Method and the Concept of the True Self

In Advaita Vedanta, a classical ancient Indian philosophical system, the core teaching revolves around

the nature of the *Atman*—the true self—and its relationship to *Brahman*, the ultimate reality. According to this philosophy, our true self is not found in our physical body, our thoughts, our roles, or even our emotions. Instead, it lies in pure awareness, or *Atman*, which is unchanging and eternal.

The *Neti Neti* method, meaning "not this, not that", is a tool of self-inquiry and negation that helps individuals peel away false identities and discover the true self. By negating all that we are not—our body, thoughts, emotions, and roles—we are left with the pure awareness that observes everything without changing.

This philosophical approach is particularly useful in philosophical counselling for individuals grappling with identity crises or existential questions. The following session illustrates the use of *Neti Neti* in helping a client explore self-identity beyond societal roles and transient emotions.

The following session illustrates how the *Neti Neti* method from Advaita Vedanta can help someone like Rohan explore his self-identity by peeling away false layers and discovering the deeper, unchanging awareness that lies at the core of his being.

Counselling Session with Rohan: Exploring Self-Identity through the *Neti Neti* Method

Rohan: [*Enters the counselling session, looking a bit restless*] I've been struggling with this overwhelming sense of confusion about who I really am. It's like I'm lost in my own life. I feel like I'm wearing a hundred different masks, and I don't know which one is really me. How do I even begin to figure out who I truly am?

Counsellor Aditi: [*Smiling gently*] It's not uncommon to feel that way, Rohan. The question "Who am I?" is one of the most profound questions we can ask ourselves. Before we go any further, though, how would you define yourself right now? How do you see yourself?

Rohan: Well, I guess I define myself by what I do—my job, my relationships, my thoughts, and my feelings. But sometimes, it feels like these things are just layers, and underneath them, there's something more... but I can't quite grasp what that is.

Counsellor Aditi: It sounds like you're already sensing that there's something deeper beyond those external identities. There's a method in Indian philosophy called *Neti Neti*, which means "not this, not that". It's a way of peeling back the layers of who we think we are, to get to the core of our true self. Does this approach resonate with what you're feeling?

Rohan: [*Intrigued*] Neti Neti... I've never heard of it. How does it work?

Counsellor Aditi: It's a process of elimination, a method of negation. We start by looking at how you currently define yourself, and we'll negate those definitions, realizing they aren't the essence of who you are. Each layer we peel back brings you closer to your true self. How does that sound to you?

Rohan: Yeah, let's try it.

Counsellor Aditi: All right. You mentioned your job first. Let's start there. Is your job who you are, or is it something you do?

Rohan: Well, no. My job is just one part of my life. I'm definitely more than what I do for a living.

Counsellor Aditi: Exactly. Your job is something you *do*, but it doesn't define the whole of who you are. But do you ever feel like your identity is heavily tied to what you do, even though you know it's just a role?

Rohan: [*Pausing*] Yeah, I do sometimes. I know I'm more than just my job, but I still feel like it's a big part of who I am. If I didn't have it, I don't know how I'd define myself.

Counsellor Aditi: That's a common feeling. Many of us identify strongly with what we do, even though it's only one part of us. So, let's acknowledge that while your job is a role you play, it's not your essence. You are not your job. [*Pauses briefly*] Neti.

Rohan: [*Nods thoughtfully*] I see what you're saying. But it's hard to let go of that.

Counsellor Aditi: Yes, it can be challenging to separate ourselves from the roles we've invested so much in. But let's continue. Now let's look at your relationships—your roles as a son, a friend, a partner. Do these relationships define your true self, or are they roles you play?

Rohan: [*Pausing to reflect*] I care deeply about the people in my life, but... yeah, they're roles I play. Sometimes I feel like there's a part of me that's separate from those roles, something more.

Counsellor Aditi: That's a good insight. Your relationships are important, but they don't fully define you. But let me ask—when you think about your relationships, do you ever feel like they're more than just roles? Like they're part of who you are at the core?

Rohan: [*Thinking for a moment*] I guess I've always thought of my relationships as part of who I am. They shape how I see myself. But I also feel like... there's more to me than just that.

Counsellor Aditi: Exactly. It's natural to feel that way. Relationships are significant, but they're still roles we play in different contexts. You're more than the roles you take on in those relationships. So, you are not just your relationships. [*Pauses*] Neti.

Rohan: [*Starting to see the pattern*] Okay, so I'm not my job, and I'm not just the roles I play in relationships. But I'm not sure what's left after that.

Counsellor Aditi: We're getting there. But let's keep peeling back the coverings. What about your thoughts and feelings? You mentioned they feel personal, more like 'you'. Are they constant? Do they always stay the same?

Rohan: No, they change all the time. I can be happy one moment and anxious the next. I might believe something today that I didn't believe last year.

Counsellor Aditi: Exactly. Thoughts and emotions are transient—they come and go. But something within you observes these changes, right? If your true self were only your thoughts and emotions, then you'd be as fleeting as they are. But you're not. So, you are not your thoughts and feelings. [*Pauses again*] Neti.

Rohan: [*Reflecting deeply*] So, if I'm not my job, my relationships, or my thoughts and feelings... then what am I?

Counsellor Aditi: That's the big question, isn't it? Let's take a look at your body now. You experience the world through your body, but is it who you really are?

Rohan: [*Pauses, considering*] My body has changed so much over the years. It feels like it's just a... vessel that I live in.

Counsellor Aditi: Exactly. Your body is a tool you use to interact with the world, but it's not the unchanging core of who you are. So, you are not your body. [*Pauses*] Neti.

Rohan: [*Quietly, almost to himself*] It feels strange... If I'm none of these things, then what's left?

Counsellor Aditi: What remains, Rohan, is awareness—the consciousness that witnesses your thoughts, your emotions, your body, and all the roles you play, yet remains unchanged. That awareness is your true self, your *Atman*. It's not something you can observe like an object, because it's the observer itself.

Rohan: [*Slowly, with dawning realization*] So... I'm the awareness that watches everything. But how can I be sure this awareness is really me? It feels so abstract.

Counsellor Aditi: That's a great question. The mind naturally seeks something concrete to hold on to. But awareness is the one thing that has always been with you—it's the part of you that hasn't changed since you were a child. By logically negating everything you are *not*, what's left is what cannot be negated—the awareness that has always been present. You can't observe it as an object because it's the subject, the one who observes. This awareness doesn't change with time, doesn't age, and isn't defined by your roles or thoughts. It simply *is*.

Rohan: [*Leaning back, a mixture of awe and contemplation on his face*] This is... so different from how I've thought about myself. It feels like I've been looking at life the wrong way all this time.

Counsellor Aditi: It's a profound shift in perspective, and it can take time to fully sink in. *Neti Neti* isn't just a concept—it's something to be experienced over time. As you continue to explore this awareness, you may begin to feel a deeper sense of peace, realizing that your true self is beyond the turbulence of life. It's always there, untouched by external chaos.

Rohan: [*Smiling softly*] I feel like I've just seen something really profound... something I'll need to sit with for a while.

Counsellor Aditi: Take your time, Rohan. This is a process of gradual discovery. When life feels overwhelming, remember to return to this process—strip away the curtains, and reconnect with the awareness that's always been there.

Rohan: [*Nodding, filled with gratitude*] Thank you, Aditi. This has been... eye-opening, to say the least.

Counsellor Aditi: I'm glad you've found it helpful. You've taken an important first step, and that's often the hardest part. I'm here whenever you want to continue this journey.

Post-session reflection: After the session, Rohan is likely to reflect on how his sense of identity has been shaped by his job, relationships, thoughts, and emotions. By realizing that these roles and feelings are not the essence of who he truly is, Rohan may begin to approach his day-to-day life with a newfound sense of freedom. As he continues this process, he might gradually detach from external validations and focus more on the awareness that remains constant, which could lead to a more peaceful and centred way of being.

Invitation to readers: As you read through Rohan's journey of self-discovery using the *Neti Neti* method, take a moment to reflect on your own life. How do you define yourself? What roles, relationships, or thoughts do you identify with? Try to take off these layers and ask yourself—who are you beyond your job, your roles, your thoughts, and your emotions? What remains when you set those aside?

After exploring the *Neti Neti* method, which helps us strip away false identities to uncover our true self, we now turn to Jiddu Krishnamurti's approach. While *Neti Neti* focuses on discovering deeper awareness, Krishnamurti extends this inquiry to how conditioned thought patterns—shaped by past experiences and fears—affect our daily lives. His philosophy encourages us to observe fear, anxiety, and conflict in relationships without judgment, revealing how these emotions are products of conditioning rather than reality. In the following sessions, we will apply Krishnamurti's insights to address these common struggles and find greater psychological freedom.

Introduction to Krishnamurti's View on Fear and Anxiety

Jiddu Krishnamurti viewed fear as one of the most pervasive forms of psychological suffering. He believed that fear arises from the mind's attachment to the past and anticipation of the future. Instead of living fully in the

present, we are often caught up in thoughts about what might happen or what has already happened, generating anxiety and inner conflict.

Krishnamurti advocated for a radical approach to understanding fear: by observing it without trying to escape, suppress, or analyse it, we can begin to see fear for what it is—a psychological construct of the mind. In doing so, we disarm its power over us. This session demonstrates how Krishnamurti's approach can be applied in philosophical counselling to help someone like Arjun confront and understand his anxiety and fear.

Counselling Session with Arjun: Understanding Fear and Anxiety through Krishnamurti's Philosophy

Arjun: [*Sits down, clearly anxious*] I've been feeling this overwhelming anxiety lately. It's like I'm constantly on edge, worried about what's going to happen next. I keep thinking about all the things that could go wrong—at work, with my family, even my health. It's exhausting.

Counsellor Aditi: [*Listening attentively*] That sounds incredibly difficult, Arjun. You've been carrying a lot of weight, constantly worrying about what could go wrong. Krishnamurti often spoke about how fear and anxiety are tied to our thoughts about the future and our attachment to what might happen. Would you be open to exploring this together?

Arjun: [*Nods slowly*] Yeah, I've heard that before—how anxiety is all in my head. But it doesn't feel like that. It feels real.

Counsellor Aditi: That's completely understandable. When we're anxious, it feels incredibly real. But Krishnamurti didn't suggest that we dismiss these feelings or try to get rid of them. Instead, he encouraged us to observe them closely—without trying to change or analyse them. Have you ever tried simply observing your anxiety, without trying to push it away or understand it?

Arjun: [*Frowns*] No, I'm always trying to get rid of it. I take deep breaths, or I distract myself, but it always comes back.

Counsellor Aditi: Most of us try to escape fear or anxiety because it's uncomfortable. But Krishnamurti believed that the first step to understanding fear is to stop running from it. Would you be willing to try something different? Instead of pushing the anxiety away, let's observe it, just as it is, without judgment. You don't need to change it—just notice it. Would you be open to that?

Arjun: [*Hesitant*] I guess I can try.

Counsellor Aditi: [*Smiling gently*] Good. Let's start by closing your eyes and taking a deep breath. Now, don't try to calm yourself down. Instead, bring your awareness to the anxiety itself. Where do you feel it in your body? Is it in your chest, your stomach, your shoulders? Just notice where it's located, and allow it to be there.

[*Arjun closes his eyes and takes a deep breath, focusing on his anxiety. After a minute, he opens his eyes, looking more thoughtful.*]

Counsellor Aditi: What did you notice?

Arjun: [*Pauses*] I felt it in my chest, mostly. It's like this tightness. Usually, I try to make it go away, but this time... I just let it sit there.

Counsellor Aditi: That's an important step. By

allowing the anxiety to just be there, without trying to change it, you begin to see it for what it is—just a sensation, a thought, not a reality. Krishnamurti believed that when we observe fear without resistance, we start to break its hold over us. How do you feel now, compared to when you first started?

Arjun: [*Thinking*] A little lighter, I guess. It didn't feel as overwhelming when I stopped fighting it.

Counsellor Aditi: That's the key. When we stop struggling against fear, we create space to understand it. Krishnamurti often spoke about how fear is tied to time—our thoughts about the future, about what might happen. What were you thinking about when the anxiety arose?

Arjun: [*Reflecting*] It was mostly about my job. I keep worrying that I'm going to mess something up, or that I'll lose my job. I'm always thinking about the worst-case scenario.

Counsellor Aditi: And that's where fear often lives—in the "what ifs" of the future. But Krishnamurti would suggest that this is a product of thought, not reality. When we live in the present moment, fear loses its power because there's nothing to anticipate or control. What if you brought your awareness back to the present, instead of being pulled into thoughts of the future? How would that change your relationship with fear?

Arjun: [*Quietly*] I guess I wouldn't be so consumed by what might happen. I'd just be here, dealing with what's actually happening.

Counsellor Aditi: Exactly. Fear and anxiety often pull us into the future, but by bringing your attention back to the present—by observing the fear as it arises—you can break that cycle. You can see the anxiety for what it is: just a thought, a reaction. Not the truth. Does that feel like something you could continue to practice?

Arjun: [*Nods slowly*] I think so. It felt less overwhelming when I just noticed it, instead of reacting to it. Maybe I've been making it worse by trying to fight it all the time.

Counsellor Aditi: That's a common experience. When we fight fear, we often intensify it. But when we observe it, we create space between ourselves and the emotion, and in that space, we find freedom. Krishnamurti believed that once we understand the nature of fear, it loses its grip on us. You don't need to control or fix it—just see it, and let it pass.

Arjun: [*With a small smile*] I think I can do that. It's different from what I'm used to, but it feels more... real, somehow.

Counsellor Aditi: It's a different approach, but it's one that can bring you closer to understanding your mind and how fear works. And as you continue to practice, you may find that fear no longer dominates your life. You'll be able to face it with clarity, rather than resistance.

Arjun: [*Nods*] Thanks. I feel like I've got something to work with now. I'll try observing it instead of running from it.

Counsellor Aditi: That's a great step, Arjun. Remember, this is a process. You don't need to rush through it. Keep observing your thoughts and feelings, and as you do, you'll start to see them for what they are—temporary, not overwhelming. I'm here whenever you need to continue this journey.

Post-session reflection:

After this session, Arjun may begin to practice observing his anxiety and fear without judgment or resistance. By shifting his focus from controlling his emotions to understanding them, he can start to see that fear is a product of thought, not reality. This practice may help him feel less overwhelmed by future uncertainties, enabling him to live more fully in the present.

Invitation to readers:

As you reflect on Arjun's session, consider your own experiences with fear and anxiety. How often do your worries revolve around future events or "what if" scenarios? Try taking a moment to observe your anxiety without trying to fix or escape it. Where do you feel it in your body? What thoughts arise alongside it? How might this practice of observation change your relationship with fear?

Introduction to Krishnamurti's Approach to Relationships

Jiddu Krishnamurti believed that relationships are a mirror through which we can observe ourselves. He argued that most conflicts in relationships arise from attachment, expectations, and conditioned responses. Rather than seeking external solutions or blaming others, Krishnamurti suggested that we should turn inward, observing how our thoughts, emotions, and conditioning shape our interactions.

Krishnamurti emphasized the importance of seeing relationships without the distortions of past experiences, judgments, and expectations. By observing our reactions to others without identifying with them, we can break free from habitual patterns of conflict and understand our own role in creating or sustaining tension. The following session illustrates how Krishnamurti's insights can be applied to help a client like Priya handle a relationship crisis by focusing on self-awareness rather than external blame.

Counselling Session with Priya: Navigating Relationship Conflict Through Krishnamurti's Philosophy

Priya: [*Sits down, clearly upset*] I'm so frustrated with my partner. We've been arguing constantly. It feels like no matter what I say or do, it turns into a fight. I love him, but sometimes I don't know if I can handle the stress anymore. We just can't seem to understand each other.

Counsellor Aditi: [*Nods empathetically*] That sounds incredibly difficult, Priya. Constant conflict can be exhausting, especially when it feels like you're not being understood. Krishnamurti often talked about how we approach relationships with so many expectations, assumptions, and past experiences that we stop seeing the other person clearly. Would you be open to exploring your reactions and emotions in this conflict, rather than focusing on the external situation?

Priya: [*Frowns*] What do you mean by that? Isn't the problem that we just don't communicate well?

Counsellor Aditi: Communication is important, but Krishnamurti believed that much of our conflict in relationships comes from our conditioned reactions—our past experiences, fears, and expectations—rather than the actual moment we're in. When we argue, we often react based on what we expect or fear, instead of seeing the other person and the situation as they truly are. Have you ever noticed how past experiences influence your arguments with your partner?

Priya: [*Pauses*] I guess sometimes I feel like I'm reacting to things that happened before. I've been in bad relationships in the past, and I don't want to go through that again. Maybe that's why I get so defensive.

Counsellor Aditi: That's a powerful insight, Priya. Krishnamurti believed that when we carry the past into the present, we distort our perception of what's really happening. In relationships, this means we're often not responding to the person in front of us, but to our fears or expectations. Would you be open to trying something different—observing your thoughts and emotions during conflict without judgment, and seeing what they reveal about your own conditioning?

Priya: [*Curious*] I've never thought about it that way. I usually just try to calm down or solve the problem. But I'm willing to try.

Counsellor Aditi: [*Smiling gently*] Let's give it a try. Close your eyes for a moment, and think back to a recent argument with your partner. As you do, notice the emotions that come up—anger, frustration, hurt. Where do you feel them in your body? What thoughts arise as you recall the argument? Don't try to fix or change anything—just observe.

[*Priya closes her eyes and takes a deep breath, reflecting on a recent argument. After a minute, she opens her eyes, looking more thoughtful.*]

Counsellor Aditi: What did you notice?

Priya: [*Reflecting*] I felt a building pressure in my chest —as if I was holding on to pent-up anger. But when I really paid attention, it wasn't just anger. There was also fear. Fear that he didn't care enough, that I'd be left alone. It reminded me of things that happened in my last relationship.

Counsellor Aditi: That's an important realization, Priya. Often, what we think is anger or frustration is tied to deeper fears—fears from the past, or expectations of what might happen in the future. Krishnamurti would say that by observing these feelings without judgment, you begin to see them for what they are—reactions shaped by conditioning, not necessarily the truth of the current moment. How do you feel about that?

Priya: [*Slowly*] It makes sense. I guess I've been bringing my past fears into this relationship without even realizing it. I'm always scared he'll leave, like my ex did. That's why I get so defensive.

Counsellor Aditi: Exactly. And when those fears come up, it's easy to react automatically, without seeing the present moment clearly. Krishnamurti believed that freedom in relationships comes from observing these conditioned reactions without identifying with them. When you recognize that these fears are just thoughts and not necessarily the truth, how does that change your perspective on the conflict?

Priya: [*Quietly*] It feels like... maybe I've been making things worse by reacting to things that aren't even happening now. I've been so caught up in my fear of being hurt again that I'm not giving this relationship a real chance.

Counsellor Aditi: That's a profound insight, Priya. When we carry our past fears and expectations into the present, we can create conflict where there doesn't need to be any. But by observing those reactions—without trying to control or judge them—you create the space to respond with clarity, rather than from old patterns. How would it feel to approach your next argument with this new awareness?

Priya: [*Thoughtfully*] I think it would be hard, but maybe it would help me not get so defensive. If I can just notice my reactions, maybe I won't feel so overwhelmed by them.

Counsellor Aditi: That's exactly it. You don't need to fix the feelings or make them go away—just observe them. By watching your thoughts and emotions without getting caught up in them, you create space to respond more calmly and authentically. Krishnamurti would say that this awareness leads to more freedom in your relationships because you're no longer bound by the conditioning of the past. Does that feel like something you'd like to explore further?

Priya: [*Nods slowly*] Yeah, I think I'd like to try that. It feels more honest—like I'm actually dealing with what's going on inside me, instead of just reacting to my partner.

Counsellor Aditi: That's a wonderful step, Priya. Relationships can be one of the best mirrors for self-understanding. By observing your thoughts and feelings, you'll gain more clarity about what's really going on beneath the surface. And as you continue this practice, you may find that your reactions start to shift, leading to more understanding and less conflict.

Priya: [*With quiet determination*] Thank you. I feel like this could really help. I've been so focused on trying to fix the relationship, but maybe I need to start with myself.

Counsellor Aditi: That's a powerful realization. By understanding yourself better, you'll naturally improve the relationship dynamic. I'm here to support you as you continue this process of self-awareness and exploration.

This session shows how Krishnamurti's philosophy can be applied to help someone deal with relationship conflicts by turning inward and observing their own conditioned responses.

Post-session reflection:

After this session, Priya may start to approach her relationship differently, observing her reactions without immediately responding to them. By recognizing that much of her defensiveness stems from past fears, she can begin to break free from these patterns and relate to her partner more authentically. Over time, this practice may lead to less conflict and greater understanding within the relationship.

Invitation to readers:

As you reflect on Priya's experience, consider your own relationships. What conditioned reactions do you bring into your interactions with others? How might your past experiences or fears shape the way you respond to conflict? Try observing your thoughts and emotions during your next conversation without judgment. What do you notice? How could this awareness shift the dynamic in your relationships?

Conclusion

In this chapter, we explored how philosophical counselling can help individuals address profound questions of identity, fear and anxiety by drawing on timeless philosophical methods such as *Neti Neti* and self-awareness. These approaches offer practical tools for self-inquiry and personal transformation, allowing clients to gain clarity and inner peace.

In the next chapter, we will dig deeper into key concepts and tools from Indian philosophy, examining how they can be applied to address contemporary issues. By exploring these ancient traditions, we will uncover practical insights that can help guide us through the complexities of modern life.

Chapter - 7

Addressing Life's Common Philosophical Dilemmas

Throughout our lives, we all face philosophical dilemmas—moments when we question the meaning behind our actions, the balance we strike in our choices, and the truths we hold. In this chapter, we'll explore some of these challenges and the insightful ways in which Indian philosophy can help us understand them. Each reflection is drawn from my academic learnings. I encourage you to engage with these ideas, applying them to your unique experiences while remaining open to alternative perspectives. Together, let's explore how these timeless concepts can offer clarity, balance, and wisdom in our daily lives.

Here I am going to address some of the most frequently asked philosophical questions and explore how Indian philosophical concepts offer insights and solutions. These timeless ideas not only provide clarity but also show us how deeply relevant they remain to the challenges we face today.

How can I find a balance between indulgence and self-denial in my life?

Striking a balance between indulgence and self-discipline is a challenge many of us face. We often find ourselves pulled between the desire for pleasure and the need for restraint. To achieve this delicate balance, consider the Middle Path, as taught by Buddhism, or Aristotle's concept of the Golden Mean. Both philosophies remind us that extremes—whether in overindulgence or strict denial—can lead to dissatisfaction. Instead, *moderation* offers a  more sustainable and fulfilling approach to life. Assess your habits and desires by focusing on creating a balance that avoids both excess and deprivation. For example, if you often find yourself overcommitting to work or losing time to distractions, setting clear boundaries between work and leisure can help you create a more harmonious rhythm in your life.

Example: You may find yourself caught in a cycle of overworking, followed by periods of guilt-ridden indulgence when exhaustion sets in. By setting intentional boundaries—allocating time for both focused work and meaningful relaxation—you can sustain your productivity while avoiding burnout. This balance allows you to recharge without the guilt of neglecting your responsibilities or your well-being.

Reflection Exercise: Consider areas in your life where indulgence or restraint has become imbalanced. Write down two or three areas where moderation could help. What steps can you take to ensure a more balanced, fulfilling approach to both your responsibilities and your pleasures?

How can I pursue my goals without becoming overly attached to the outcomes?

Once you've embraced moderation, another challenge often emerges: how can you strive toward your goals while remaining detached from the outcome? To do this,  embrace *Nishkama Karma* from the *Bhagavad Gita*. This concept encourages focusing on the act itself rather than on the results. By putting full effort into your tasks while letting go of specific expectations about success or failure, you cultivate a calm, peaceful mindset. This approach reduces anxiety and helps you find satisfaction in the process of your work, rather than being tied to its outcome.

Example: Imagine you are working on a project that means a lot to you. Instead of worrying about whether it will be a success, focus on doing your best with each step. This way, the process itself becomes fulfilling, and you reduce the stress that comes from an overemphasis on results.

Reflection Exercise: Think of a goal you are currently working toward. How would your approach change if you focused solely on the effort, without worrying about the result? Write down your thoughts on how detaching from the outcome might bring you more peace and focus.

How can I make balanced decisions when faced with conflicting opinions?

In our everyday lives, we often encounter situations where we're besieged by conflicting opinions—whether at work, in relationships, or in broader societal debates. These moments can make it difficult to make clear, confident decisions. How do you weigh opposing viewpoints without feeling overwhelmed or stuck?

A useful tool for handling this is *Syadvada*, a concept from Jain philosophy. *Syadvada* teaches that truth is not absolute but context-dependent. This means that different perspectives can each hold a part of the truth, depending on the circumstances. By acknowledging that multiple viewpoints may have validity,  you avoid the trap of rigid thinking and can approach decisions with more openness and balance. This approach helps you appreciate the complexity of real-life situations and prevents the need to see things in black-and-white terms.

Example: Imagine you're involved in a team project at work. One colleague argues for prioritizing efficiency to meet a tight deadline, while another emphasizes the importance of quality, even if it takes more time. Both perspectives have merit depending on the situation. Instead of dismissing one in favour of the other, *Syadvada* encourages you to recognize the value in each, helping you make a decision that balances both efficiency and quality, taking into account the full picture.

Reflection Exercise: Think about a situation in your life where you've been faced with conflicting opinions—whether at work, with family, or in a personal decision. How could you view these differing perspectives as complementary rather than oppositional? Write down how embracing the idea that both can hold truth might lead to a more balanced and informed decision.

How can I determine what is true or reliable when faced with conflicting information?

In a world overflowing with information, it can be hard to know what to trust, especially when you encounter conflicting viewpoints. How can you figure out what is true or reliable? The concept of *Pramana* from Indian philosophy provides a clear framework for assessing the validity of information.

The first method is perception (*Pratyaksha*)—what you directly observe with your senses. The second is inference (*Anumana*)—using logical reasoning to draw conclusions from the evidence you have. The third is testimony (*Shabda*)—relying on credible sources or expert opinions. By applying these three methods, you can analyse conflicting information more critically and arrive at a clearer, more reliable understanding of the truth.

Example: Suppose you read two contradictory articles about a new medical treatment. First, use *Pratyaksha* by gathering observable facts from both articles. Next, apply *Anumana* by logically evaluating the data presented—does one argument follow from the evidence better than the other? Finally, use *Shabda* by considering the reliability of the sources—are they well-regarded experts or questionable sources? This process will help you cut through the confusion and make a more informed judgment.

Reflection Exercise: Think of a recent time when you encountered conflicting information, whether about health, news, or work. Try applying the three methods of *Pramana*. How did perception, inference, and credible testimony guide you toward a clearer understanding? Reflect on how these tools helped you distinguish what was more likely to be true.

How can I deepen my understanding of the nature of reality and integrate this understanding into my daily life?

Understanding the nature of reality is one of the deepest philosophical questions. But how do we integrate that understanding into everyday life? To explore this, follow the steps of *Sravana* (Listening), *Manana* (Reflection), and *Nididhyasana* (Meditation) from Vedanta philosophy. First, immerse yourself in philosophical teachings. Next, reflect on what you've learned, comparing it with your own life experiences. Finally, meditate on these insights, allowing them to become part of your daily perspective. This process helps you bridge philosophical wisdom with real-life actions, making profound concepts practical and meaningful.

Example: If you're studying the concept of impermanence, reflect on how this idea appears in your life—perhaps in the changing nature of relationships or the shifting of seasons. Meditate on this to internalize the insight and adjust your perspective.

Reflection Exercise: Take a teaching or concept that has influenced you recently. Reflect on it through meditation or journaling. How can you apply this understanding to your daily interactions or choices? Write down one or two ways this insight could reshape your worldview or actions.

How can I align my actions with my true self and purpose in life?

Once you've deepened your understanding of reality, you may ask: How can I live in a way that truly reflects who I am and what I'm meant to do? The concept of *Svadharma*—rooted in ancient Indian philosophy, particularly in the *Bhagavad Gita*—offers a guiding principle. *Svadharma* refers to "one's own duty" and emphasizes living in alignment with your unique nature, talents, and the role you play in society. It's about understanding your strengths and values, and then shaping your actions around them. When your actions are in tune with your deeper self and contribute positively to those around you, you experience a greater sense of authenticity and fulfilment. By living according to your *Svadharma*, you create a life driven by purpose.

Example: Let's say you're working in a job that pays the bills but doesn't resonate with your passions or values. Over time, this disconnect might leave you feeling unfulfilled. Reflect on whether this work reflects your true abilities and aspirations. If not, it might be time to explore roles or activities that align more with your natural skills and inner calling, even if that means taking small steps toward a career or lifestyle shift.

Reflection Exercise: Take a moment to reflect on your strengths, talents, and core values. Are the actions and responsibilities in your life aligned with these aspects of your true self? Identify one area where you could shift your focus or make a change to bring your life more in line with your *Svadharma*.

How can I manage distractions and focus on my inner self?

In today's world, distractions are everywhere—whether from technology, social media, or the constant noise of daily life. Staying connected to your inner self amidst this can be challenging. The practice of *Pratyahara*, rooted in Yoga philosophy, offers a solution by teaching the withdrawal of attention from external distractions. This involves consciously turning your focus inward, away from the constant bombardment of stimuli.

Example: Try setting aside just one hour each day to disconnect from all devices—turn off your phone, step away from social media, and create a quiet space. During this time, focus on breathing exercises, journaling, or simply sitting in silence. This practice can help clear the mental clutter caused by constant notifications and external noise, giving your mind the rest it needs to regain clarity. Over time, this practice helps you build a stronger connection to your inner world, fostering peace and balance.

Reflection Exercise: Consider the distractions that most often pull you away from your inner focus, such as social media, TV, or general noise. Make a plan to minimize or eliminate these distractions for a day or a week. Afterward, reflect on how reducing these distractions impacted your ability to reconnect with yourself and whether you noticed any changes in your mental clarity or sense of calm.

How can I understand the nature of change and the continuity of existence in my life?

Change is one of the few constants in life, yet it can be difficult to understand and accept. How do we make sense of change while also finding a sense of continuity? *Pratitya-samutpada* (dependent origination) from Buddhist philosophy offers a way of understanding this. It teaches that everything arises from a web of interconnected causes and conditions. Nothing in life exists in isolation; everything is linked to something else.

On the other hand, *Kshanabhanga-vada* (momentariness) explains that everything is constantly in flux—nothing stays the same from one moment to the next. When you accept that change is both natural and inevitable, you develop the ability to adapt and embrace the present, rather than clinging to things that are passing. This understanding of interconnectedness and impermanence helps you become more resilient and open to life's transitions.

Example: Think about how relationships evolve over time. The dynamics between friends, family, or partners shift as people grow and circumstances change. By recognizing that these changes are natural and inevitable, you can better adapt and accept these transitions, instead of resisting or holding onto how things used to be.

Reflection Exercise: Reflect on a recent change in your life—whether personal, professional, or relational. How does viewing this change through the lens of dependent origination and momentariness affect your understanding of it? Think about how accepting the transient nature of life might help you cope with change in a healthier, more adaptable way.

While we've explored several key tools from Indian philosophy, it's important to acknowledge that this tradition offers a wide range of timeless and profound methods. Due to space limitations, I've focused on just a few concepts to show how they can help address modern challenges. These selected concepts offer practical guidance, but they are just a glimpse into the vast wisdom Indian philosophy has to offer, including tools and concepts such as *Tarka* (reasoning), *Vada* (dialogue aimed at establishing truth), *Anvikshiki* (critical inquiry or reflective analysis), *Upaya* (skilful means), *Sthitaprajna* (steadiness of wisdom), *Ahimsa* (non-violence), *Aparigraha* (non-possessiveness), *Vairagya* (detachment), *Upeksha* (equanimity) and so on.

As we move forward, our focus will shift to the challenges and criticisms of philosophical counselling. By examining the concerns and reflecting on its limitations, we can gain a clearer understanding of where philosophical counselling stands today and how it might evolve to better meet its potential, as well as the needs of those seeking its guidance.

Chapter - 8

Major Criticisms and Challenges of Philosophical Counselling

Philosophical counselling offers deep insights into life's big questions but is not above criticism. As the practice grows, concerns are raised about its credibility and effectiveness. Key criticisms include the lack of scientific evidence, unclear methods, and insufficient training standards. In this chapter, we'll explore these issues and look at how philosophical counselling can improve to better serve clients and become a more recognized practice.

1. Lack of Empirical Evidence:

One of the central criticisms is the absence of empirical studies proving the effectiveness of philosophical counselling. Psychological counselling benefits from years of research and evidence-based practices, whereas philosophical counselling relies more on subjective dialogue and reasoning. Advocates of philosophical counselling assert that its value lies in qualitative rather than quantitative outcomes. The subjective nature of philosophical dialogue, they argue, is difficult to measure but no less impactful. Clients often report feeling more self-aware and in touch with their values, which may not fit neatly into traditional psychological metrics. Proponents argue that philosophical counselling should be evaluated on its own terms—by how well it helps clients navigate philosophical, existential and ethical dilemmas, not just by measurable symptoms.

2. Arbitrariness of Methods and Tools:

Philosophical counselling lacks standardized methods, which can make the practice feel arbitrary. Counsellors use different approaches based on their backgrounds, so sessions can vary widely. This can leave clients unsure of what to expect, raising concerns about the reliability and effectiveness of the counselling.

3. Lack of Training and Skill Assessment:

Unlike psychologists or therapists who undergo rigorous training and licensing, philosophical counsellors do not always follow standardized training processes. This can lead to concerns about whether they are properly equipped to handle complex client issues. For instance, one counsellor might have extensive academic training in philosophy but little experience with real-world counselling, while another might have practical experience but limited philosophical depth. The absence of formal assessments means clients cannot be assured of consistent competency. This might raise concerns about whether all counsellors are prepared to handle complex emotional or existential issues.

4. Blurred Boundaries with Psychological Practices:

Another issue is the potential overlap between philosophical counselling and psychotherapy. The risk here is that philosophical counsellors, who are not trained to handle mental health issues, may venture into areas like anxiety or depression without the proper expertise. A counsellor might try to help a client work through these emotional difficulties using philosophical frameworks when, in fact, the client may need psychological or psychiatric care. This overlap can potentially harm clients who need more specialized intervention.

Advocates stress that philosophical counselling isn't intended to replace therapy. Instead, it's designed to address different issues—mainly existential, ethical, and philosophical questions that go beyond mental health concerns. When done correctly, philosophical counselling focuses on helping clients navigate life's big questions rather than addressing psychological disorders. Proponents also emphasize the importance of knowing when to refer clients to a mental health professional if deeper psychological issues emerge.

5. Legalization and Licensing:

The absence of regulation in philosophical counselling means anyone can offer services without proving qualifications. This lack raises concerns about the quality and safety of the counselling provided. For instance, without a legal framework, individuals offering philosophical counselling may not be held accountable for malpractice or unethical behaviour. Licensing would help establish clear standards and ensure that counsellors are qualified to work with clients, providing an extra layer of trust and professionalism. Clients would benefit from knowing their counsellor has met certain qualifications, much like in the field of psychotherapy or psychiatry.

6. Need for More Research:

To address these criticisms, philosophical counselling needs more research. Studies could help validate its effectiveness and create clearer guidelines for practice and training. This would help the field gain recognition and establish it as a legitimate option for personal growth and self-understanding. Additionally, research could help distinguish philosophical counselling from psychological practices, helping to clarify its uniqueness. By investing in research, philosophical counselling can build a more solid foundation, ensuring its long-term growth and credibility.

Conclusion:

Addressing the challenges and criticisms are crucial step for its evolution. These criticisms also present opportunities for growth. By investing in more research, developing clearer training standards, and establishing a regulatory framework, philosophical counselling can solidify its place alongside more traditional therapeutic practices. Rather than seeing its lack of structure as a weakness, the field can embrace its flexibility while working toward a more professionalized and trustworthy framework. As research evolves and boundaries are clarified, philosophical counselling has the potential to complement more traditional therapeutic practices and offer clients a unique form of intellectual and personal guidance.

In the next chapter, we will turn our attention to the future of philosophical counselling in India. We'll examine how philosophical counselling can adapt and flourish within the Indian context, offering meaningful solutions to the unique challenges faced by individuals in modern society.

Chapter - 9

Conclusion: The Future of Philosophical Counselling in India

Philosophy for the Modern World

In today's fast-changing world, the need for philosophy is more pressing than ever. But what does this truly mean? Should it remain confined to the academic domain, where abstract and theoretical debates take place? Or should it take a more practical turn, engaging with the real challenges that individuals face in their daily lives? Who determines what kind of philosophy society needs, and more importantly, what kind of philosophy do we as individuals require? Reflecting on these questions helps us understand the unique role philosophical counselling can play, particularly in India, where philosophical traditions are rich but underutilized in modern therapeutic practices. To understand the future of philosophical counselling in India, we must explore how it intersects with existing fields such as psychotherapy, psychological counselling, and psychiatry, and how it can offer something distinct in guiding individuals through life's complexities.

Reconnecting Philosophy with Society:

Historically, philosophy was central to public life. However, over time, it has retreated into academia, becoming increasingly theoretical and disconnected from everyday concerns. The global philosophical community has been shrinking as fewer people see its relevance to their lives. To reverse this trend, we must reconnect philosophy with the concerns of everyday life. Philosophical counselling aims to break the stereotype that philosophy is purely academic. The idea of "Philosophy at work" offers a way forward, combining theoretical wisdom with practical tools that address real-world issues. It brings philosophy out of the classroom and into the lives of individuals. By integrating reflective, practical insights into counselling, we can show how philosophy can be used to address life's challenges. Utilizing platforms like blogs, social media, newspapers, and public talks can help promote philosophical thinking and make it accessible to a wider audience.

Philosophical Counselling in India: Opportunities and Challenges

India, despite its rich philosophical heritage, has seen little development in the practice of philosophical counselling. Globally, philosophical counselling has gained traction in America and European countries, where dedicated organizations promote it as a distinct profession. For example, the American Philosophical Practitioners Association (APPA) has over 500 members across 46 states, while Holland, with a population of 6.5 million, has over 100 practitioners.

One notable effort to popularize philosophical counselling in India is the work of the Philosophical Practitioners Association of India (PPAI), founded by philosophical practitioners such as Prof. Balaganapathi Devarakonda, Dr. Vikas, and others. The PPAI seeks to build a community of philosophical practitioners who are committed to making philosophy relevant to everyday life. Their vision is to bring philosophy back into the public sphere by offering it as a tool for personal and societal growth.

However, philosophical counselling in India faces several challenges. Unlike psychotherapy or counselling psychology, philosophical counselling is not yet a widely recognized profession. Efforts to build awareness, establish certification programs, and create a framework for professionalization are still in their infancy. Additionally, there is a need to address the cultural and societal resistance that exists within both the academic community and the general public. There is limited public awareness, and even within academia, philosophical counselling is sometimes viewed with scepticism. Revitalizing philosophical communities, such as the one that once existed in Rajasthan, and promoting interactive workshops, seminars, and training programs can help to build momentum for the practice. The goal is to make philosophical counselling an integral part of both academic and non-academic life in India.

Professionalization and Legalization

For philosophical counselling to flourish in India, the practice must undergo a process of professionalization and legal recognition. Currently, the field lacks standardized certification and formal licensing, which can lead to inconsistency in the quality of services provided. Establishing a regulatory framework will not only raise the standards of practice but also offer clients greater confidence in the legitimacy of philosophical counselling.

Legalization of the practice will also help protect clients by ensuring that only qualified practitioners offer services. This process requires building a professional association that advocates for recognition at the governmental level and creating ethical guidelines.

Conclusion

The future of philosophical counselling in India is full of potential. As individuals seek greater meaning and clarity in an increasingly complex world, the demand for philosophy's practical applications will only grow. By drawing on both India's philosophical heritage and modern global insights, philosophical counselling can become a vital part of the country's mental health and wellness landscape. The rise of digital platforms also presents an exciting opportunity for philosophical counsellors to reach broader audiences through online sessions and workshops.

However, the journey toward professionalization and legal recognition is not without challenges. To establish philosophical counselling as a respected field, we must raise public awareness, integrate with other mental health professions, and work toward building a regulatory framework that ensures high-quality practice.

The vision is clear: a future where philosophical counselling is not just an academic or niche practice, but a mainstream profession that addresses life's most profound philosophical and ethical questions. Ultimately, the future of philosophical counselling will depend on ongoing research, professionalization, and a willingness to bridge the gap between academic philosophy and everyday life.

Further Readings

(Curated For Beginners)

Articles

Achenbach, G. B. (1998). On Wisdom in Philosophical Practice. *Inquiry: Critical Thinking Across the Disciplines, 17*(3), 5–20. https://doi.org/10.5840/inquiryctnews199817322

Achenbach, G. (2001, June). Philosophische Praxis Führt Die "Lebenskönnerschaft" Im Schilde. *6th International Conference on Philosophical Practice.*

Blass, R. B. (2008). On the Possibility of Self-Transcendence: Philosophical Counseling, Zen, and the Psychological Perspective. *Journal of Chinese Philosophy, 23*(3), 277–297. https://doi.org/10.1111/j.1540-6253.1996.tb00631.x

Devarakonda, B. (2021). Shifts in the Classical Indian Conception of Philosophical Practice: *Vedic, Itihāsa-purāṇic,* and *Dārśanic. Philosophical Practice, 16*(1), 2602-2609.

Devarakonda, B., Baniwal, V., & Garg, V. (2023). Conversations on Psychological Counselling and Philosophical Counselling: Examining the Convergences and Divergences Between Philosophical and Psychological Counselling. *Philosophical Practice, 18*(1), 3072-3084.

Grimes, P. (1997). Philosophical Midwifery: A Method of Socratic Inquiry. *Philosophical Practice Journal, 3*(2), 233-240.

Lahav, R. (1995). What Is Philosophical in Philosophical Counseling? *Journal of Applied Philosophy, 13*(3), 1-14.

Lahav, R. (2001, March). Philosophical Counselling as a Quest for Wisdom. *Practical Philosophy.* Retrieved from http://www.practical-philosophy.org.uk

Mehuron, K. (2010). Philosophical Practice in a Psychotherapeutic World. *Philosophical Practice: Journal of the American Philosophical Practice Association, 5*(3), 661-684.

Mills, J. (2013). Philosophical Counseling as Psychotherapy. In E. D. Cohen & S. Zinaich Jr. (Eds.), *Philosophy, Counseling, and Psychotherapy* (pp. 101-112). Newcastle: Cambridge Scholars Publishing.

Nagaraj, N., & Ramakrishnan, M. (2022). Philosophical Counselling: Foundations and Functions. *Quest Journals: Journal of Research in Humanities and Social Science, 10*(11), 368-372.

Raabe, P. B. (2004). Morals and Ethics in Philosophical Counselling: Sex, Suicide, and Mental Illness. *Journal of Philosophical Practice*. E-journal of the University of St Paul, University of Ottawa, Canada.

Sulavikova, B. (2014). Key Concepts in Philosophical Counselling. *Human Affairs, 24*(4), 574-583.

Sulavikova, B. (2012). Questions for Philosophical Counseling. *Human Affairs, 22*(2), 131-141.

Books

Carr, N. (2010). *The Shallows: What the Internet Is Doing to Our Brains*. W. W. Norton & Company.

Cohen, E. D. (2003). *What Would Aristotle Do? Self-Control Through the Power of Reason*. Prometheus Books.

Ellis, A. (2001). *Overcoming Destructive Beliefs, Feelings, and Behaviours: New Directions for Rational Emotive Behaviour Therapy*. Prometheus Books.

Eyal, N. (2019). *Indestructible: How to Control Your Attention and Choose Your Life*. Ben Bella Books.

Frankl, V. E. (2006). *Man's Search for Meaning*. Beacon Press.

Hanh, T. N. (1999). *The Miracle of Mindfulness: An Introduction to the Practice of Meditation*. Beacon Press.

Howard, A. (2000). *Philosophy for Counselling and Psychotherapy: Pythagoras to Postmodernism*. Palgrave Macmillan.

Kabat-Zinn, J. (1994). *Wherever You Go, There You Are: Mindfulness Meditation in Everyday Life*. Hyperion.

Marinoff, L. (2000). *Plato, Not Prozac! Applying Eternal Wisdom to Everyday Problems*. Harper Collins Publishers.

Marinoff, L. (2001). *Philosophical Practice*. Academic Press.

Nelson, L. (2010). *Socratic Method and Critical Philosophy: Selected Essays* (T. K. Brown III, Trans.). Kessinger Publishing, LLC.

Newport, C. (2019). *Digital Minimalism: Choosing a Focused Life in a Noisy World*. Portfolio.

Nikhilananda, S. (1949). *Katha Upanishad*. Sri Ramakrishna Ashrama.

Nussbaum, M. C. (2003). *Upheavals of Thought: The Intelligence of the Emotions*. Cambridge University Press.

Phillips, C. (2002). *Socrates Café: A Fresh Taste of Philosophy*. W. W. Norton & Company.

Singer, M. A. (2015). *The Surrender Experiment: My Journey into Life's Perfection*. Harmony Books.

(Sorted For Advance Learners)

Articles:

Buck, W. (2009). Welcome to My Philosophy Class. *Philosophy Now, 71*.

Coliva, A. (2009). Notes on Italian Philosophy, Peer-Reviews and "La Corruttela". *Philosophia, 38*(1), 29-39.

Cohen, M. (1919). A Slacker's Apology. *New Republic, 21*(261), 19-20.

Farneti, R. (2009). A Minor Philosophy. *Philosophia, 38*(1), 1-28.

Farneti, R., & Ferrara, A. (2012). What is a Minor Philosophy? A Conversation on Thinking from the Periphery in a Global World. *Philosophia, 40*(4), 717-739.

Glock, H. (2008b). Analytic Philosophy and History: A Mismatch? *Mind, 117*(468), 843-865.

Gutting, G. (2012, February 19). Bridging the Analytic-Continental Divide. *New York Times: Opinionator*. Retrieved from http://opinionator.blogs.nytimes.com/2012/02/19/bridging-the-analytic-continental-divide.

Haldane, J. (1999). Thomism and the Future of Catholic Philosophy. *Faithful Reason: Essays Catholic and Philosophical* (pp. 3-13). Routledge.

Haldane, J. (2001). The Diversity of Philosophy and the Unity of Its Vocation. *Faithful Reason: Essays Catholic and Philosophical* (pp. 31-41). Routledge.

Hankey, W. (2006). 9/11 and the History of Philosophy. *Animus, 11*. Retrieved from http://www2.swgc.mun.ca/animus/Articles/Volume%2011/Hankey.pdf.

Kaufman, D. A. (2006). Knowledge, Wisdom and the Philosophy. *Philosophy, 81*(1), 129-151.

Kidd, I. J. (2012). Humane Philosophy and the Question of Progress. *Ratio, 25*(3), 277-290.

Kitcher, P. (2011). Philosophy Inside Out. *Metaphilosophy, 42*(3), 248-260.

Koopman, C. (2010). Bernard Williams on Philosophy's Need for History. *Review of Metaphysics, 64*(1), 3-30.

Maxwell, N. (2012a). Arguing for Wisdom in the University: An Intellectual Autobiography. *Philosophia, 40*(4), 663-704.

Maxwell, N. (2012b). In Praise of Natural Philosophy: A Revolution for Thought and Life. *Philosophia, 40*(4), 705-715.

McCann, H. (2003). Philosophy in America at the Turn of the Century. *APA Centennial Supplement, Journal of Philosophical Research.*

O'Hear, A. (2001). Editorial: What Philosophy Is. *Philosophy, 76*(1), 1-2.

Outlaw, L. T. (1996). The "Future" of Philosophy in America. *On Race and Philosophy* (pp. 183-204). Routledge.

Pieper, J. (2006). What Does it Mean to Philosophize? In B. Wald (Ed.), R. Wasserman (Trans.), *For the Love of Wisdom: Essays on the Nature of Philosophy* (pp. 27-80). Ignatius Press.

Putnam, H. (1997). A Half Century of Philosophy, Viewed From Within. *Daedalus, 126*(1), 175-208.

Quine, W. V. O. (1979). Has Philosophy Lost Contact with People? *Theories and Things* (pp. 190-193). The Belknap Press of Harvard University Press.

Read, R. (2010). On Philosophy's (lack of) Progress: From Plato to Wittgenstein (and Rawls). *Philosophy, 85*(333), 341-368.

Rorty, A. O. (2008). The Dramatic Sources of Philosophy. *Philosophy and Literature, 31*(1), 11-30.

Rorty, R. (1980). Philosophy in America Today. *Consequences of Pragmatism: Essays, 1972-1980* (pp. 211-230). University of Minnesota Press.

Schwatz, N. (1994). Philosophy as Blood Sport. *Philosophy as Blood Sport.* Retrieved from http://www.sfu.ca/~swartz/blood_sport.htm.

Sosa, E. (2011). Can There Be a Discipline of Philosophy? And Can It Be Founded on Intuitions? *Mind & Language, 26*(4), 453-467.

Striker, G. (1999). Why Study the History of Philosophy? *Harvard Review of Philosophy, 7,* 15-18.

Wilhelmsen, F. D. (1987). The Great Books: Enemies of Wisdom. *Modern Age, 34*(3/4), 323-331.

Williams, B. (2000). Philosophy as a Humanistic Discipline. *Philosophy, 75*(4), 477-496.

Books:

Beyer, C., & Burri, A. (2007). *Philosophical Knowledge -- Its Possibility and Scope*. Rodopi.

Cottingham, J. (2009). *The Fine, the Good, and the Meaningful.* The Philosophers' Magazine.

Dummett, M. (2010). *The Nature and Future of Philosophy*. Columbia University Press.

Ganeri, J., & Carlisle, C. (Eds.). (2010). *Philosophy as Therapeia*. Royal Institute of Philosophy Supplement, 66(1).

Gilson, E. (2011). *Methodical Realism* (Reprint). Ignatius Press.

Glock, H. (2008a). *What is Analytic Philosophy?* Cambridge University Press.

Hadot, P. (1995). *Philosophy as a Way of Life*. Wiley-Blackwell.

Leiter, B. (2004). *The Future for Philosophy*. Oxford University Press.

Maritain, J. (2005). *An Introduction to Philosophy* (E. I. Watkin, Trans.). Rowman & Littlefield.

O'Hear, A. (Ed.). (2001). *Philosophy at the New Millennium*. Royal Institute of Philosophy Supplement, 48.

O'Hear, A. (Ed.). (2010). *Conceptions of Philosophy*. Royal Institute of Philosophy Supplement, 65.

Peperzak, A. T. (2006). *Thinking: From Solitude to Dialogue and Contemplation*. Fordham University Press.

Sallis, J. (2007). *The Verge of Philosophy*. University of Chicago Press.

Williamson, T. (2007). *The Philosophy of Philosophy*. Blackwell.

Index

("*f*" means "following pages")

A

Achenbach, Gerd	37, 49, 51
Ahimsa (Non-violence)	92
Analytical Stage	58, 63
Anvikshiki (Critical Inquiry)	92
Aparigraha (Non-possessiveness)	92
Aristotle (Golden Mean)	85
Ashtavakra Gita	34
Authenticity	10, 55 *f*, 63 *f*, 90
Absurdity (life's meaning)	2

B

Bhagavad Gita	31, 33 *f*, 39, 41, 86, 89
Brahman	67
Brihadaranyaka Upanishad	32
Breaking Free from Autopilot	12
Buddhist Dialogues	34
Buddhist Text *Milinda-Panha*	35

C

Casuistical Method	46
Cognitive Behavioural Therapy (CBT)	23 *f*, 29
Comparative Stage	61, 64
Consciousness	2, 34 *f*, 39 *f*, 54, 71
Contractarian Approach	48
Critical Stage	60, 64
Critical Thinking Approach	43

D

Dependent Origination (*Pratitya-samutpada*)	91, 92
Dialectical Behaviour Therapy (DBT)	25
Dialectical Method	39
Directive Methods	50

E

Edification Approach	45
Emotional Regulation	25 *f*, 44
Equanimity *(Upeksha)*	92
Existential Dialogue	55
Existentialism	15, 61

G

Grimes, Pierre	36 *f*, 54

F

Freedom and Responsibility	56
Financial Success vs. Fulfilment	18, 25
Future of Philosophical Counselling	97 *f*, 101

I

Indian Philosophy (*Darshanas*)	31

J

Journaling	14, 89, 91

K

Katha Upanishad	32, 41, 104
Krishnamurti, Jiddu	4, 73 *f*
Kshanabhanga-vada (Momentariness)	91

L

Lahav, Ran	20, 38
Logotherapy	53
Logic-Based Therapy (LBT)	50, 52 *f*
Legal Recognition	100, 101

M

Manana (Reflection)	89
Marinoff, Lou	21 *f*, 38, 104
Middle Path (Buddhism)	85
Mindfulness Practice	13, 14
Moral Dilemmas	14, 29, 33, 43, 46, 47
Mortality	32, 41, 56

N

Neti Neti Method	67 *f*, 72 *f*, 83
Neuroscience	11
Neuroplasticity	9
Nididhyasana (Meditation)	89
Nishkama Karma (Desireless Action)	86
Non-directive Methods	49, 56

P

Philosophical Counselling in India	31, 66, 97 *f*
Philosophical Midwifery	37 *f*, 50, 54, 102
Phenomenological Analysis	54, 55
Philosophy as a Way of Life (Darshana)	36
Prefrontal Cortex	14
Psychoanalysis and Psychodynamic Therapy	23 *f*, 29
Psychological Counselling	20 *f*, 94, 98, 102

R

Rational Emotive Behavioural Therapy (REBT)	24
Reconnecting Philosophy with Society	98

S

Self-awareness	7, 11, 21, 34, 42, 56, 59, 67, 78, 82 *f*
Self-discovery	3, 5, 7, 22, 24, 45, 79, 54, 67, 73
Socratic Method	36, 49, 51 *f*
Sravana (Listening)	89
Stoicism	15, 36
Sthita-prajna (Steadiness of Wisdom)	92
Syadvada	87
Synthetic Stage	59, 63

T

Tarka (Reasoning)	92

U

Upanishads	31 *f*, 34, 38 *f*
Upaya (Skilful Means)	92

V

Vada (Dialogue aimed at Truth)	92

S

Self-awareness 7, 11, 21, 31, 32, 36, 53, 57, 78, 82 ?
Self-discovery 3, 5, 7, 12, 14, 15, 19, 54, 67, 78
Socratic Method 36, 49, 51 ?
Sutuna (Listening) 58
Stoicism 15, 36
Sthita-brajna (Steadiness of Wisdom) 54
Svadhada 87
Symbolic Stage 60, 65

T

Tarka (Reasoning) 57

U

Upanishads 37, 78, 80 ?
Upaya (Skillful Means) 92

V

Vada (Dialogue-oriented Debate) 57